WHISKERS IN THE WILD
SAVING AND SOCIALIZING COMMUNITY CATS

DEBRA BLAINE

This book is a combination of personal experience, anecdotal evidence, scientific research, and consultation with cat experts. However, under *no* circumstances should anything in this publication be taken as veterinary advice for cats or medical advice for humans, nor is it a substitute for legal counsel.

Furthermore, the author and publisher take no responsibility for injuries resulting from trapping or handling cats, whether they be homeless or house cats. The guidelines in this book are suggestions only, and each person is responsible for fully educating themselves and maintaining safe standards. It should be understood that no one can ever guarantee the behavior of an animal.

Copyright © 2025 by Debra Blaine

All rights reserved.

No part of this book may be reproduced in any form or by any electronic or mechanical means, including information storage and retrieval systems, without written permission from the author, except for the use of brief quotations in a book review.

ISBN eBook: 979-8-9926615-1-4

ISBN paperback: 979-8-9890985-9-0

US Copyright registration pending

Published by Very Indie Press, Melville, NY

www.veryindiepress.com

*For my Father
and
all the little Leos who have adopted me over the years,
especially Midnight.*

And for All Cats, Everywhere.

PRAISE FOR WHISKERS IN THE WILD

"Dr. Blaine has an amazing gift. She has captured all the fine points of feline behavior through her extensive research. Her experiences are heartwarming, entertaining, and educational. Every cat lover will love Whiskers in the Wild."

— Dr. Mitchell Kornet, DVM
   Medical Director, Mid Island Animal Hospital, Hicksville, NY
   Midislandvet.com

CONTENTS

Forward by Rachel Geller, Ed.D.	ix
Introduction	xi
1. THE HISTORY OF OUR RELATIONSHIP WITH CATS	**1**
Big Cats and... Not-So-Big Cats	1
From Deity to Devil	2
Contemporary Cats	5
What *is* the difference between a feral, a stray, and a house cat, anyway?	6
2. COMMUNITY CATS	**9**
Medical Maladies	11
Feral Versus Stray Behavior	12
Feeding Community Cats	14
Cat Shelters	16
How to Know if a Cat Needs Medical Attention	17
The Role of TNR	18
3. READING CAT BEHAVIOR	**20**
Body Language	21
Vocalizations	25
Whiskers at Work	29
Can You/Should You Bring Any Cat Indoors?	30
4. TO CATCH A CAT	**32**
Snap Traps, aka Humane Box Traps	33
Drop Traps	36
Cameras	39
Catch Pole Nets	39
Catching a Community Cat with Your Hands	40
No Kit-Napping!	41
8 Steps to Trap a Cat	42

5. CAT'S OUT OF THE BAG	44
From Bushes to Cushions	44
Getting to Know Your Cat	45
The Power of Play	48
Bringing Two Cats Together	52
Declawing—*Don't!*	54
Setting Limits	55
6. REAL RESCUES BY JOHN DEBACKER	57
Oakley	58
Merry	59
Wanda	61
House Fire	62
Metro	64
Ettore	65
7. THE BENEFITS AND OPPORTUNITIES THAT COME WITH BEING ADOPTED BY A CAT	68
Perks	68
How to Make Your Cat Like You	70
Communicating with Your Cat	72
Exploring All Options	75
8. IT TAKES A VILLAGE	78
9. FUN FACTS ABOUT CATS	83
Acknowledgments	89
About the Author	93
Dr. Rachel Geller	95
John DeBacker	97
Dr. Marge Goldin	99
Also by Debra Blaine	101
End Notes	103

FORWARD BY RACHEL GELLER, ED.D.

Cats have always been my passion. They are part of my life in a way that only other cat lovers can understand.

We cat parents have certain things in common. We share our homes, garages, yards, and other indoor and outdoor spaces with our felines because we love them. We want these animals to be safe, happy, and healthy. If this book can play a role in achieving that result, it will have met its goal.

There is a common belief that cats are solitary creatures who do what they want regardless of human care and intervention. That is a myth. It is indeed possible to help cats, to modify their behavior, and for humans to become involved in cats' lives. But we need to take our time to understand the root causes of feline behavior and each one's individual history and temperament. Every cat is different, just like every human is different. Factors such as the age of the cat, their health, how they were previously treated by humans, and many influences we have no way of knowing about all play a role in that cat's perception of and how she responds to the world.

Realistically, cat rescuers, fosters, and adopters cannot know every facet of a cat's life before they encounter them. The goal of this book is to provide an understanding that will help improve the lives of the cats we find ourselves sharing spaces with and caring about.

I hope this book makes cats an even bigger part of your world. It's a journey well worth taking.

INTRODUCTION

It was a frigid winter afternoon, and I had just stepped outside to bring food to an ailing neighbor when I saw her: a little black-and-white Tuxedo, sitting in the frozen dirt behind the currently leafless bushes that lined my house.

"Oh. Hi," I said.

We stared at each other for half a minute, and I started to shiver.

"Meow."

It was the most plaintive yet *polite* sound I'd ever heard come from an adult cat, and I've been caring for cats for more than forty years.

"Hi," I said again, balancing the boxed food and navigating the house keys into my pocket without taking off my gloves. The wind gusted and nearly blew my package out of my hands. The sky was gray, and the smell of snow foretold the coming blizzard.

"Meow."

"Well," I said, "I have to bring this to Bonnie, but I'll be right back. I mean, if you want to wait."

I walked three houses down to my friend and helped her unpack the food. She'd broken her right arm, so simple things had become rather tricky. We chatted for a few minutes, long enough for me to wonder whether the little stray would still be outside. After all, we had no history together, although I did recall seeing her occasionally roaming the community. I later discovered that someone down the street had been feeding her off and on for around five years.

As I walked back up my driveway, there she was, still sitting in the same place. Looking cold and forlorn.

"Are you hungry?"

"Meow."

It was the only word she knew.

"Okay... give me a minute," I said.

I left the inner door open as I went to get her something to eat, and she sat looking through the storm door. Her nose left a smudge mark on the glass.

She practically inhaled a large can of cat food followed by a bowl of kibble, as if she hadn't eaten in a week—which I later learned was exactly the case. And thank God. The snow started that evening, and as first winter storms in New York sometimes do, it raged into a tempest that shut down Long Island for thirty-six hours.

Two days later, my feline friend was back, and thus started a new relationship. Despite the objections of my muted Tortie, who is part Persian, part Maine Coon, part Ragdoll, and 100 percent pampered darling, I bought a small outdoor shelter for the front porch and fed the little kitty twice a day. She, in turn, began to eat treats from my hand and, after a couple of months, would purr away while I petted her gingerly. As long as I didn't move too fast or try to put *two* hands on her at the same time. She was terribly skittish, interpreting any sudden movements as potential threats. Her back and face were solid black except for a single narrow white streak down the center of her nose.

I named her Midnight.

Until January 31, 2021, I had no experience with community cats. All my four-legged companions had come from rescue shelters (or the pound, as we used to call it, where unclaimed animals may be put to death). I didn't know the difference between a stray and a feral, and I assumed my daily visitor had been in a terrible fight because the top of her left ear looked like it had been chewed off. I had no idea what Trap-Neuter-Return, or TNR, was or how tragic and widespread the plight of hordes of homeless cats is.

In this book, I hope to share the travails of those who cannot speak for themselves and help educate anyone who wants to be part of their salvation. Whether or not you can adopt a homeless soul or two into the warmth of your home (as I ultimately did with Midnight), tend to them outside in the wild, or donate funds to offset their veterinary bills, understanding their needs and the culture of cats is the first step.

To be clear, the majority of truly feral cats *should* stay outside. They are not accustomed to human touch, and they are fairly adept at finding their own food and caring for their families. Bringing them in and trying to force socialization on them is a chore for us and a hardship for the cats. That doesn't mean they don't have needs. Our civilized society, by its very nature, both attracts them with the promise of discarded food and endangers them with technology.

Moreover, there is also no way we can find homes for all the prowlers out there, even if they wanted to come inside. Shelters are filled to capacity as it is.

That said, whoever spayed and returned little Midnight to the backwoods should have their head examined. My little sweetie never belonged outside. Perhaps, like in so many situations, there simply wasn't room for One. More. Cat.

At least she is in her forever home now. And she inspired this book.

INPUT FROM PROFESSIONALS

I'm enormously thankful to the people who have contributed to this reference guide. Dr. Rachel Geller, EdD, a renowned expert in cat behavior, generously shared her wisdom about how to successfully introduce stray cats into our homes and to our other cats, and was an indispensable resource for Chapter 5, "Cat's Out of the Bag."

Dr. Marge Goldin, DSW, is an experienced volunteer trapper with Tender Loving Cats. She both sent me literature and personally explained capture procedures and types of traps in great detail, providing most of the material for Chapter 4, "To Catch a Cat." Marge was also invaluable for getting Midnight into a carrier one fateful day in August 2021. Without her help, I fear that gentle soul would still be fighting to survive "in the wild."

Long Island's famed cat crusader, John DeBacker, describes several of his rescue operations in Chapter 6. He gives us a bird's-eye view of the more dramatic techniques he's used to extricate desperate animals from harrowing circumstances, often saving lives against all odds—and, occasionally, at risk to his own. However, let it be known I do *not* recommend that anyone emulate his stagecraft by putting their own lives in danger.

Sadly, not every rescue attempt has a happy ending, and there are always a few tragedies alongside the victories. It is a fact of life that the vast majority of true ferals wandering the backs of bakeries would *not* pounce on the opportunity to reserve a seat on your sofa. However, they do appreciate food and a warm shelter. The more cats multiply, the more little mouths there are to feed, and the fewer safe harbors are available to them.

This is why the TNR program, which traps, neuters, and returns cats to their neighborhoods, is so important.

Consider this: One female cat can have two to four litters a year. If each litter produces five kittens, well... do the math. When these innocent babies struggle, whether from hunger or injury, we just don't have enough resources to save them all. Even though cats have become a favorite household companion worldwide, there aren't enough homes for all the kittens born, and many suffer horrible deaths right in our backyards.

WHO AM I TO TALK?

I'm a human doctor, not a veterinarian. However, my vet always talks to me like a colleague, for which I am exceedingly grateful, and he explains the differences in physiology between humans and felines (or canines). Understanding these subtle nuances helps me make the best decisions regarding the health of my four-legged family members.

I'm also a certified professional coach and master trainer, which assists me in understanding how feelings translate into action. Primarily on the part of people, but in fact, cats experience many of the same emotions that we do.[1]

If I could coach cats, I would. Although perhaps it's the cats who should be coaching us...

I've had pets in my family for sixty years, and I dare say, I often preferred their company to many people I know. Through dedicated, albeit informal study, I've made it a point to learn about their behavior and needs and have reaped the rewards of the unconditional love they shower on their chosen human confidants. It is devastating when they leave us, hopefully from natural causes, but I always try to consider that it would be far worse if we died first and left them alone; they'd be lost without us. At least we can be there to help them make their final transition.

Until I entered into the world of stray and feral rescues, I had no idea how many despicable humans abandon their animals—their *family members*—by dumping them on the streets, leaving them behind in an apartment they move out of, or abusing them until the little critters have no choice but to run away.

I started exploring animal psychology nearly thirty years ago, when, for the first time as an adult, I had both a dog and a cat. An orange Tuxedo had hitched a ride in the wheel well of a truck and was dropped off at a dog rescue in Queens, New York. I met that tiny kitten when I was inquiring about dog training for my Golden Retriever. Have you ever tried to discipline a dog when your five-year-old thinks everything the puppy does is hysterically funny? My little boy's cackles were a far more powerful reinforcement than any treat or admonition I could give, and they occurred with every act of mischief on the part of the dog.

So I'd already been learning about dog behavior when the new kitten came along, and they had their own unique relationship—one I needed to figure out. SunshiDog died at the age of thirteen from lymphoma, and by then, twelve-year-old Zilly had been hiding for years. Had I only known about Jackson Galaxy, I could've made his life so much happier, but alas, it was 1998, and the inspirational TV series *My Cat from Hell* did not air until 2011. After Sunshi died in 2009, Zilly finally came out of the closet and had a bright life until his kidneys failed at age sixteen. But I still feel the guilt.

SammieKat was only eight weeks old when I introduced her to the family, and she was a big part of Zilly's emotional rehabilitation. But watching the grumpy Zill-meister and the fearless, mischievous kitten was not only entertainment, it was also a lesson in cat interactions. Wouldn't you know, due to Sam's persistence, they became best friends, and years later, Sammie sat with Zilly during his hospice period, her tail draped over him while he slept. This bonding process was certainly facilitated by my having gotten a kitten. Another adult cat would have provoked new territorial issues that a two-pound furball did not.

After Zilly passed, I did not get another cat until Midnight showed up. I wrongly assumed that after a period of transition, bringing these two cats together would go as swimmingly as it had before. Except this time, not only were they both already adults, but I also did not understand that due to their dissimilar histories, they prowled in completely separate social circles.

From kittenhood, both Zilly and Sammie grew up indoors; that gave them some common ground. While I'm quite certain Midnight was once a beloved house cat, she had been on the streets for years. She had different expectations of her environment and people, and did not gain confidence in her new surroundings so easily.

Behaviorally, they were as dissimilar as a prep school–educated billionaire and a pauper from the back streets of New York City, or so I was told by an animal communicator I enlisted when trying to broker better relations between them. It made sense.

We never know what has befallen the homeless, and I can only guess at the torture little Midnight lived through. She can't tell me, but I've seen evidence. Two bullets from a pellet gun were seen on x-ray, and she was terrified of men when I first brought her in. Her emotions were in a constant state of tug-of-war, craving my love yet fearful of human touch. After four years together, I still can't pick her up for hugs, but for all that, Midnight is exceptionally loving and remains the only person in my life who is *always* happy to see me. Always. She'll stop eating and run to my side when I walk in, just to share some affection.

Since being adopted by my little stray, I've learned an enormous amount about the lives and behaviors of cats, indoors and out, alone and together, their instincts and their distinct personalities—and their social circles.

I also discovered what to do—and what *not* to do—when contemplating trap and rescue: how to prepare for capture, where you'll bring the little mouser once they're caught, and further, how to introduce them to your current resident feline if you are keeping the cat. It's been an incredible journey, and I've met some amazing humans.

Selfless, generous humans, who will not stand by and watch a creature as intelligent, heartful, and in many ways psychologically similar to us suffer.

CHAPTER 1
THE HISTORY OF OUR RELATIONSHIP WITH CATS

BIG CATS AND... NOT-SO-BIG CATS

FELINES of all sizes seem to have an air of mastery, mystery, and majesty about them. Their independent manner, prestige as quintessential hunters, and penchant for being impeccably groomed no doubt contribute to that notion. Each species has different needs and different practices, but when it comes down to basic behavior, a cat is a cat is a cat.

The smaller members of the *Felis* genus, the ones we take into our homes, may get labeled as aloof, uncooperative, destructive, or untrainable, but this is unfair. They are just more autonomous and are decidedly *not* born to serve like their canine counterparts. It's one more way they are psychologically akin to humans.

> *A cat will be your friend, but never your slave.*
> —Theophile Gautier

Let's be clear: Cats are not dogs. Many people expect their feline family to react the way their canines do, which can only lead to frustration. Dogs were bred to work alongside humans, and they have an innate desire to please us. But much like the dog's wolf ancestors, felines do not have this predisposition.

Just like we don't want someone telling us what to do all the time or putting their hands all over us whenever *their* mood strikes, cats feel the same. Despite the fact that they are indeed a highly social and affectionate species, they need their space, physical and mental, so when they enter into a relationship with us, it's on their terms. Yes, even after they become family. Although, from personal experience, I believe they make many concessions to our needs—so long as we respect theirs.

The category of big cats includes lions, tigers, leopards, cheetahs, and their large cousins. All those magnificent felines that sit proudly on top of the food chain. They thrive on six continents and in climates as diverse as the African deserts, the tropics, and the snowy tundra. They are a remarkably adaptive species.

The smaller cats we see in our neighborhood are not so comfortably situated in the circle of life. They have their own animal predators, like coyotes, wolves, and other cats vying for food; birds of prey; and, of course, abominable humans. However, if you share your home with a cat (and I assume many of you do), you've no doubt recognized the occasional haughtiness or pride that all cats are known for. They often seem to act like royalty. Lionhearted if not lion-sized.

FROM DEITY TO DEVIL

The history of the human-cat relationship is fascinating. Believe it or not, we've had a symbiotic relationship for over ten thousand years, beginning in Mesopotamia.[2] That area, also known as the Fertile Crescent, is situated between the Mediterranean Sea and the Persian Gulf and is thought to be where the first agricultural communities arose. In other words, since civilization began, cats and humans have interacted.

As the early settlements started storing grain for leaner times, local rodents arrived, unable to resist capitalizing on these new feasts.

Anyone who's ever had to deal with a mouse in their house—which can quickly become a whole nest—knows how resistant mice are to barriers, able to squeeze into the tiniest of spaces. They were a nemesis to farmers.

However, those pocket-sized mammals made a tasty treat for the African wildcats (*Felis silvestris lybica*) who came to prey on them and thereby became something of a hero. Cats of all sizes are carnivores (or meat eaters), so these wildcats posed no threat to the fields of wheat, barley, and beans, but they performed admirably in the pest control department. In addition, they likely chased away snakes and other dangerous vermin. It was a match made in heaven.

African wildcat

Even though cats were and are fully capable of prospering on their own, over time, they habituated themselves to the presence of humans, and somewhere along the way, the relationship developed into mutual appreciation and companionship.

But they were not just welcomed.

Have you ever heard the joke, "Dogs think they're human but cats think they're God?" It's actually rooted in history.

Whether we convinced them of that or they gave us the idea, there's no way to tell for sure. But in some cultures, cats were exalted.

Dating back to antiquity, cats found their way into mythology and were revered in cultures across Asia and the Middle East. Killing a cat in ancient Egypt was a crime punishable by death, and several deities were depicted with catlike attributes. These forms appear both in art and in some mummifications that were buried alongside the pharaohs.

Perhaps the most well known is Bastet, the goddess of pleasure, protection, fertility, motherhood, and good health. She is painted with the body of a woman and the head of a cat,[3] but there were others, and India and China had gods and goddesses in their lore that took the shape of cats as well.

The skillfulness of the cat as predator no doubt played a part in achieving their privileged status, and perhaps their persnickety attitude contributed. Nevertheless, I'm sure you're aware they can also be extraordinarily loving. Even today, being chosen by a cat is considered an honor, and in some societies across Asia and Europe, it's thought to be a good omen.

Cats accompanied us when we migrated from Asia to Europe and ultimately, to the Americas. Unfortunately, their presence in Europe was less venerated for a period of time.

With the advent of Christianity, there was a move to abolish all pagan rituals, and the feline connection to other gods made it sacrilegious to associate with them. Many so-called witches were burned at the stake along with their familiars, their cats who were thought to have the ability to change shape and generally bring about evil.

So, when the bubonic plague hit Europe, it was an easy jump to blame the spread of the disease on cats, which increased society's inclination to torch them. This did nothing to stall the pandemic, however, since *Yersinia pestis* was carried and transmitted by the class of fleas that infest rats. Nevertheless, felines fell further into disfavor.

It wasn't until the late 1800s, when Queen Victoria befriended a couple of Russian Blues and kept them at her royal court, that their standing changed and it was once again in vogue to be friends with a feline.[4]

Meanwhile, their talent as excellent exterminators blended well with the needs of mariners who voyaged across the ocean. As prolific procreators, cats multiplied and colonized America right along with the early Pilgrims. Kittens were sometimes gifted or sold to sailors, farmers, ranchers, and shopkeepers for their dual role in pest control and companionship.

All that notwithstanding, cats were never bred for their temperaments or to excel in certain tasks like dogs were. We liked them just the way they are—a point felines agree with, I'm sure. Their unusual features evolved by mating with other species in the *Felidae* family, including a variety of wildcats. Some studies show that today, cats are the most popular pets in the world, perhaps owing to the invention of kitty litter in the 1940s, which made it reasonable to bring these noble creatures indoors. Presently, we tend to value them less for mousetrapping and more for their unmatched love and devotion. But if you have a colony of cats living in your backyard, chances are you won't have any voles creeping into your house.

CONTEMPORARY CATS

I mentioned how resilient the species is. One surprising thing I noticed is how Midnight's hair is so much softer and smoother now that she's been indoors for a few seasons. She literally feels like a different cat. These remarkable animals actually change their coats to suit the climate—but that doesn't mean your typical *Felis catus*, or the homeless mouser ferreting out a few rodents in your garden, is safe in subzero temperatures without shelter.

Snow leopards have intrinsically longer, thicker, and denser fur than our community friends. Even when the weather turns cold and our outdoor cats grow extra padding under a coarser coat as Midnight did, they are not nearly as well equipped to handle the dropping temperatures and can suffer serious illness if they don't find shelter.

And unlike those apex predators, the modern domestic cats roaming our neighborhoods must constantly balance their instincts to behave like a hunter one minute and like prey the next. Consequently, they are expert escape artists as well as skilled trackers.

It's been said that humans domesticated dogs but cats domesticated themselves, and not only is it essentially true but their DNA has not changed much from that of their ancestors thousands of years ago.[5] The sweetest house cat is merely one generation away from becoming a feral animal. This is why determining whether a homeless cat is a true feral or simply a stray defines how to approach them and what to expect from their behavior once trapped.

Many say that a feral will never adapt to being a house pet, while others have recognized that while this is commonly the case, each cat has a distinct personality and generalizations should be made cautiously. One thing is absolute: It won't happen overnight, and it requires enormous patience on our part. And further, it may not always be in the best interest of the cat.

photo credit: Oscar Fickel

WHAT *IS* THE DIFFERENCE BETWEEN A FERAL, A STRAY, AND A HOUSE CAT, ANYWAY?

Genetically, not much. Behaviorally, a lot. A feral cat was born outside, has never known a human's touch, hunts their own food when no human patrons are available, and has likely scouted out a sheltered environment under a porch, in an abandoned shed, or a hollowed-out tree in the woods. She may also be part of a larger colony. Cats have been living successfully in the wild for centuries.

A stray is either lost or abandoned, a house cat who once had a home. Maybe a warm fireplace, loving affection from a favorite human, and the security of daily food and toys to play with.

Until tragedy struck.

It could be that their human became ill or died, and the surviving family turned the little moggy out. It could be that one day, the person adored by the little feline decided they didn't want their furry friend anymore, or needed to move and coldheartedly left the cat behind. Or perhaps one member of the household abused them to the point that they needed to run. Unlike ferals, strays have to relearn how to survive.

These are the saddest. The ones who've been betrayed. For a while, they may still be looking for love and affection, but as years go by, they slip further and further into feral character. Trying to piece together their histories is both frustrating and heartbreaking.

Some super friendly prowlers in your neighborhood may be indoor-outdoor pets who qualify as house cats, since they are cared for, generally have a loving family, and have all their needs met. But it is not recommended to let your kitty roam like this. He will be subject to the many dangers confronting all cats in the wild, including altercations with other animals.

When ferals belong to a colony, it tends to be a multigenerational family whose members support one another. Drifter cats who approach these groups are frequently chased away, especially if resources are scarce.

My little Midnight was obviously a stray when she came to my door. She had people skills, for one thing. She meowed at me, and adult cats *only* meow to humans; they do not meow to each other. So if the cat you're feeding on your patio talks to you, it's a pretty safe bet that they once had a human family.

It's incredible that despite having been kicked to the curb—possibly literally—some strays still long to find kindness among us. My tiny Tuxedo is one of those. When I inquired in my community, I discovered a woman down the block had been feeding her off and on for years, and although Midnight was never comfortable going inside, my neighbor had been able to pet her and even applied medication to repel ticks and fleas.

Unfortunately for her beneficiary, this warmhearted animal lover began to travel more, spending weeks at a time out of state. Which was why the hungry little stray wandered over to my doorstep.

After I brought Midnight inside—a story I'll share a little later—she began peeing blood, and I brought her to the vet.

Midnight had bladder stones that were surgically removed. But I'll never forget my veterinarian calling me at work as she was being evaluated. I'd never heard him so angry, and he'd been caring for my pets for two decades.

"Where did you say you got this cat?" he asked.

I repeated that she arrived at my front door one day, and he told me my neighbors had been shooting her!

Well, I don't believe the close-knit community I live in did any such thing, but I am sure that Midnight moved—I certainly would have. The x-ray that revealed the stones in her bladder also uncovered two pellets embedded in her body. One in her right thigh, a few millimeters from her femur, and the other in her belly, not far from her spine and her aorta. She could have been crippled—or killed. How in the world did this little kitty keep faith that she would find a compassionate human somewhere?

Midnight teaches me every day to never give up, even when all seems lost. Sanctuary could be just around the corner.

For all that, getting her—or any community cat—into your home or to a doctor for medical care is not easy. Even your fluffy house cat doesn't generally walk into the carrier voluntarily, and they trust you. Every puddy I've ever had—and until Midnight, I'd had each of them since kittenhood—has complained bitterly when I put them into a carrier.

That makes things complicated, because if you are bringing an outdoor cat into your house with other resident pets, it's very important that you have your vet check the newcomer over first so they don't spread any illness to your existing furry family members.

- When cats enter into a relationship with us, it's on their terms.

CHAPTER 2
COMMUNITY CATS

Rocco

THE TERM COMMUNITY cats refers to all cats who live exclusively outside. Distinct from the big cats like those who roam the safari or the Himalayan foothills, those you see behind your favorite restaurant and the pets you adopt from your local shelter are called domestic cats, or *Felis catus*. And like their wildcat predecessors, they are known for their reclusive nature. However, although they hunt alone, feral cats live in stable social groups as long as the food supply is sufficient.[6] Lost or stray cats who are not born into a colony will generally be found prowling alone as they forage for food and shelter.

So, are cats solitary or social beings? The answer is, they are both. Cats are "selectively social" and fairly particular about who they'll bond with—just like we humans are. This holds true in both indoor and outdoor environments.

Don't try to put cat behavior into a dog's template. Feline social structure is looser than their canine counterparts, whose wolf ancestors traveled in packs. There is no clear ranking of each animal in these *clowders*, which is another name for a cat colony. The concept of an alpha male or female, designating dominant or submissive roles as we label dogs, does not really apply.

If resources are scarce, fights over food can lead to injury, but otherwise it's rather personality differences that tend to dictate who gets the lion's share of the first feed. When skirmishes occur, cats typically resolve conflict with avoidance by backing off or leaving the colony. This same tactic shows up indoors. Your cat may hide or simply distance himself from the family if he's feeling stressed, though if he feels intruded upon, he's liable to defend his territory.

Outdoor colonies are usually families surrounding the mother, called the queen or molly, and can include several generations. The female relatives help keep watch and may even nurse other cats' kittens when the queen goes out to hunt.

Fathers do not play a role in kitten care, and more commonly leave the group when they mature. Colony members all know one another and recognize strangers who may try to join them, so unless food is abundant, a newcomer will not be welcome.[7]

Although cats have been thriving outdoors for centuries, the modern era brought new challenges. Besides their natural predators, they must now contend with automotive traffic, construction machinery, and the viciousness of some human beings.

MEDICAL MALADIES

When survival amenities are insufficient or territory is in dispute, conflicts between cats may lead to debility or the spread of disease. If a molly is either incapacitated, cannot find enough food, or illness spreads to the family, the kittens are at high risk.

The average lifespan of an outdoor cat with no human support is generally estimated to be about two to five years. However, studies cited by Alley Cat Allies and the Feral Cat Spay/Neuter Project have found that free-roaming cats can live much longer with interventions such as feeding, neutering, vaccinating, and medical care when needed.[8] Our indoor mousers often make it to fifteen and beyond.

Aside from the jeopardy of being run over by a car, poisoned by insecticides, or wounded by industrial machinery, a variety of viruses and secondary infections due to injury can sicken colony cats who generally don't have access to a local vet.

Feline leukemia virus (FeLV) and feline immunodeficiency virus (FIV) are unique to cats (humans can't catch them) and are transmissible through saliva, so if they bite each other during a brawl, they can pass the infection along. While there is no cure, the concomitant illnesses that result can often be managed with regular veterinary treatment. Don't be alarmed, the incidence of these illnesses is low, estimated at only 4 percent.[9] In fact, it is so low that many shelters do not even test for it when performing TNR.

There is also the danger of rabies, which affects the central nervous system and is always fatal without prompt immunization. That virus can infect multiple species, including us, and poses a serious danger, since the animal suffering from this sickness becomes maddened and may attack indiscriminately and without provocation. If you see *any* animal acting overly aggressive or foaming at the mouth, back off and call your local animal control service immediately.

But rabies in cats is very rare, and there have not been any cases of a person contracting rabies from a cat in decades.[10] Furthermore, cats can be immunized against both rabies and FeLV, and the widespread practice of vaccinating our pets has kept this virulent disease mostly in check. One animal you always need to watch out for is bats; they carry the virus without becoming ill themselves. If you find a bat anywhere in your home, everyone of every species needs immediate vaccination, whether you think it bit you or not.

All three of these contagions are transmitted through saliva, but other, less dramatic illnesses can more commonly plague community cats by affecting their respiratory, skin, and gastrointestinal systems, for which they may also need medical care.

Despite their acclaimed employment history on farms and sailing ships, today's ferals are frequently seen as a neighborhood problem, with some towns instituting laws against feeding them. And yet the homes fortunate enough to have a clowder of mousers in their backyard have little to worry about from rodents. Cats even hunt insects.

When my son was fourteen, he didn't want to go back to summer camp, so I told him he had to get a job. He worked a few days a week at the local bakery and commented one day that there were mice in the back near the ovens. He said they used to have a few cats living behind the store, but the owner had shooed them away.

"They should have kept the cats," I said, "but if the mice are prospering, at least you know there are no rats."

Aren't cats a more palatable pest control service than rats?

FERAL VERSUS STRAY BEHAVIOR

Because a fully feral cat was born outside and has never formed a friendship with a human, they are wary of people. They see us as potential predators who move too fast, are unpredictable, and are bigger and stronger than they are. Perhaps they've had to bear the brunt of disgusting antics, like being used as target practice or tortured for kicks. There are such despicable people out there. As a result, many shelters will not offer black cats for adoption around

Halloween, since some sick minds want them only for the holiday and will then turn them out or worse after the festivities pass.

Kittens can usually be socialized, but age and even the former status of the parents come into play. Studies show that if the father was a house cat or the mother once trusted people, then the kitten is more likely to accept human touch than if the lineage has lived outside for multiple generations.[11] Furthermore, the longer a stray cat remains in the wild, the more feral she becomes. All this means that it becomes more difficult to bring these cats indoors. It takes patience and perseverance to gain an animal's trust.

Making eye contact is seen as a sign of aggression in the animal world, and feral cats will avoid doing so unless preparing for a confrontation. Ferals may also show fearful posturing, like crouching low to the ground, piloerection (hair standing up tall), and tail tucked around or beneath them; their ears may be flat or twitching. If you feed them regularly, they'll probably start to relax and trust you a little, look you in the eyes, and allow you to come closer, but many unsocialized cats will never allow a human to touch them.

On the other hand, some stray cats still exhibit residual indoor behavior. They may parade their tails high or curled at the top into a question mark, which denotes confidence and friendliness, and they'll more readily make eye contact with you. Still, you must go slowly. If you want to make friends, offer food and *always let the cat come to you.*

By sitting down, you reduce your size and therefore your potential threat in the moggy's mind, and if you offer a hand, never approach from over the cat's head, as he may interpret that as intent to hurt him. Either palm up low to the ground or perhaps extend a single finger.

The feline equivalent to a handshake is to sniff each other with their noses, but it would be unfortunate to present your face close to an unknown prowler for such a greeting—nor would it likely be taken as the overture of friendship you intended. The back of your loosely held fist is a safer invitation for her to come give you a snuff. I'm sure you know that if you become family, it's not uncommon for house cats and their human companions to touch noses.

Most feline communication occurs through smell, which puts us at a notable disadvantage. We cannot register, much less recognize, the spectrum of pheromones they rely on. Have you ever seen your furry companion standing with their mouth open slightly? Not only do they use their noses, but they have an additional vomeronasal, or Jacobson's organ, in the roof of their mouth through which they can send supplementary, more precise information directly to the olfactory centers of the brain. They literally *taste* the scent in the air.

Another distinction that I previously mentioned is that adult feral cats do not meow—which is not to say they don't vocalize. Kittens will mew to their mamas for attention, but meowing is a practice that cats have developed specifically to communicate with humans. They realize that we rely on speech, so they learn to accommodate us—if they choose to be in our company. If a community cat meows at you, though they may now be unsocialized, there's a better chance they'll soften up to humans.

Chapter 3 includes information on cat vocalizations and their meanings, along with body language.

FEEDING COMMUNITY CATS

All healthy felines are accomplished predators, but the availability of chow can vary by season. As the cat population grows exponentially through unchecked breeding, the food they find may not be sufficient to support their numbers. Birds and mice are scarcer in winter, and all mammals need more calories to survive in the cold. Think of yourself waiting at the bus stop in February, stomping your feet or rubbing your hands to warm your body. This requires energy. When it's cold out, cats need to move more too. So if you can feed them a little extra, they will be grateful, even if they don't visibly express their gratitude. I mean, they are cats, right?

Cats instinctively avoid stagnant water, so give them wet food with lots of gravy in the summertime to keep them hydrated, and in winter, when they need those extra calories, it's a good idea to drop a few spoonfuls of kibble on top of or next to their canned cuisine. If you already feed them dry cereal, they'll need more of it.

I have a neighbor who used to buy a barbeque chicken every week to supplement her daily visitor's menu, and he scarfed it up. But you don't need to go to such lengths, especially if you're feeding multiple cats. Also, be careful about what table food you feed them. Garlic, onions, some nuts, raisins, and chocolate are potentially toxic to felines—and canines too.

When putting out food, keep the dish as flat as possible. Plates (paper is fine) are better than deep bowls. When those sensitive kitty whiskers rub against the sides of a container, it can be irritating, causing "whisker fatigue."

Please note: If you start feeding a cat or cats, they will expect you to continue. Sudden cessation is heartbreaking. If this is a stray, it's undoubtedly yet another betrayal.

Furthermore, cats, like humans, feel most secure with routine. So if you can provide their meals on a relatively uniform schedule, they'll be outside waiting for you when you show up with their grub.

Some will say we shouldn't feed these colony cats at all, perhaps even chase them away (as did the owner of the pastry shop my son worked at that summer). But nature abhors a vacuum. The colony settled *here* because there were resources to support them. If you chase this clowder away, it's a sure bet that another family will move in. And the next tenants might be a much less desirable neighbor—they might not even be cats.

CAT SHELTERS

Cats are mammals, which means they're warm-blooded. Perhaps that's stating the obvious, but another neighbor of mine, an intelligent man who loved the friendly kitty who frequently came to visit him, assumed that weather was never a problem because, he said, "Cats are cold-blooded." They are not. In fact, they can get frostbite on their ears, paws, and noses.

Some cats are better outfitted for the cold, like a Maine Coon, but all can suffer when the wind chill drops below freezing, so providing shelter can be lifesaving. Outdoor cat houses come in various sizes and are relatively inexpensive. I found them online, ranging from under $30 up to $180, and for $450, you can get a full cattery, a multilevel unit designed for several cats to live enclosed but outdoors. Whatever you choose, get them digs that will comfortably fit the number of cats who will be using it. Too much space, and it will get drafty, and with too little, somebody will be stuck outside.

If you want to spend less money, you can make a shelter yourself out of Styrofoam coolers, plastic storage containers, or wood. Give the dwelling both a front and a back door to allow for a quick escape, which will make the animal feel more secure. Some handy cat-loving  carpenter types advertise homemade cat houses on social media that may be more to your liking and easier on the wallet. Straw (not hay) will insulate them and keep them relatively dry. If you get confused, use the mnemonic: Straw is for strays, hay is for horses.

The house I bought for Midnight was about $40 and had two exits, so she would never be trapped inside. It came with a divided clear plastic flap over each doorway to keep the wind out. I put it on my front porch, and she lived in that refuge all winter, safe from wind, rain, and snow. Some items come with heating pads you can plug in, or you can get a self-heating mat that reflects the animal's warmth back at them.

HOW TO KNOW IF A CAT NEEDS MEDICAL ATTENTION

Feral cats fall prey to many illnesses and injuries. Fights over food between cats or other animals, like raccoons or coyotes, may result in visible injuries, and sometimes their curiosity has them sticking their noses into perilous places where they don't belong. See John's story in Chapter 6 about a cat whose head was wedged in a plastic container for days.

Bleeding or secondary infection of lacerations is usually easy to spot from a distance, and sometimes a limp will tip you off that the cat needs medical care. But often, wounded or sick animals will crawl off by themselves to hide from predators, and you may have no idea where they are or even that they need help. If you've been caring for an outdoor cat for a while and know their habits, a change in behavior, appetite, or demeanor may be a sign of systemic illness. If your regular caller suddenly disappears, search for hiding places that would suit an injured animal.

I asked my vet about the pellets he found in Midnight. How did she survive without treatment? He told me these are usually incidental findings, and the animal usually crawls off and hides until they either heal—or die.

If you're confronted with an injured mouser, you have a conundrum. Getting a community cat to a veterinarian is a project that generally requires trapping. No matter the relationship you have with your little furball, they're unlikely to let you pick them up and put them in a carrier. Heck, my SammieKat resists that, and she's been my BFFF (Best Feline Friend Forever) for fifteen years. See Chapter 4 on trapping to learn how you can handle this yourself and when you should ask for help.

THE ROLE OF TNR

> *One cat just leads to another.*
> —Ernest Hemingway

TNR, or Trap-Neuter-Release, is a humane way to serve the outdoor cat community. By limiting the number of pregnancies, cats have more available resources, and it saves lives in the long run.

It may sound harsh to sterilize innocent animals, but according to the Humane Society, the mortality rate of feral kittens is more than 75 percent in their first few weeks of life.[12] The queen will look for a safe, isolated place to deliver, but if she later feels threatened, she will try to move her newborns to a different nest, since she must step away to forage for food. That leaves her kittens at the mercy of other animals and makes it difficult for us to find her den to rescue her babies.

When a cat is taken for TNR, they are spayed or neutered, and most also receive rabies and FVRCP vaccinations (Feline Viral Rhinotracheitis, Calicivirus, and Panleukopenia), and deworming medication. Not only does this help stabilize the population of feral cats, but they will be healthier in their outdoor homes. The left ear is tipped, meaning a half centimeter is trimmed off the top of the pinna, so they can be recognized from a distance as having already been managed. This makes it clear that they do *not* need to be trapped again.

When I first met Midnight, I thought she'd been attacked because part of her ear was missing. I understand it's necessary to identify those who have already been spayed or neutered, but it still breaks my heart that her ear was cut. However, I can vouch for the fact that it has obviously healed without lingering discomfort. My otherwise skittish little girl lets me rub her ear with absolutely no sign of pain and makes no attempt to turn her head away.

- Even though all felines are fairly self-sufficient, community cats have challenges in our industrialized world. Providing food, shelter, and medical care lengthens their lives and reduces their suffering.
- TNR helps keep the feral population in check, limits competition for food and shelter, and prevents kittens from suffering sad, needless deaths. The net result is healthier cats living in greater harmony with the human population.

CHAPTER 3
READING CAT BEHAVIOR

FELINE BEHAVIOR HAS NOT BEEN STUDIED AS meticulously as their canine counterpart's. Dogs are social beings at heart; their wolf ancestry is rooted in the pack mentality, where leadership hierarchies, teamwork on the hunt, and communal raising of pups are ingrained. So, when we humans step into the role of pack leader, dogs already understand this and more readily accept our authority as an alpha figure.

On the other hand, the domestic cat descends from solitary creatures who voluntarily latched onto human societies for *reciprocal* gain. In order to make this affiliation work, we've both had to put in some effort. Mutual understanding is at the heart of all relationships, and that means learning how to meet each other's needs.

While we predominantly use words to get our messages across, felines do not. Their primary channels are through smell, sound, and body language, and they are excellent communicators—once we understand how to decipher their communiques. You might be surprised to learn that their vocalizations are far more advanced than those of a pooch.

In addition to their huge repertoire of auditory cues, cats use their bodies to send memos. Of course, so do dogs, but a wagging tail from your friendly Labrador has a whole different meaning from your Tabby's tail whipping back and forth, and woe to he who does not know that.

Complex discussions would be revealed if we could tune into the world of pheromones, the odors left by either urine or scent glands when a cat rubs on an object. Our brains cannot detect pheromones, much less interpret them, and although we can certainly smell urine, we cannot decipher the information that an individual tomcat's or molly's emiction reveals.

Both of these types of markings give vital information about the cat who left them: their gender, whether a queen is in heat, plus a code by which kittens can track their mommas. The scent profile of each cat is unique, just as each of us humans has a distinct smell (deodorant notwithstanding). Felines leave a trail of data from glands located on their cheeks, forehead, paw pads, lips, tails, and anus, to name a few.

Given that we are not likely to go around sniffing the trees in our community, and unless rankled, undomesticated animals typically do not vocalize *to us*, let's start with the visual cues they provide. From the feline perspective, they should be adequate to clearly convey whether our company is appreciated or not.

Jackson Galaxy is known for reminding us that everything about a cat's behavior and physiology relates to their survival, whether as predator or prey.[13] If we look at feline behavior in this way, it will make it easier to understand what they are telling us.

BODY LANGUAGE

Tails. Tails are the easiest thing to observe on a cat and are an important indicator of a cat's mood. Unlike socialized cats, most ferals will keep their tails lowered when they're walking. If they held them up high, it would be like waving a flag to potential enemies or the morning snack they're stalking, saying, "Here I am, over here!"

If a cat's tail is held straight out behind them, they are feeling

 explorative but cautious. In general, the lower the tail, the more vigilant they are, and when the tail is all the way down, tucked to the side of their body, or between their legs, that's a clear sign that they're frightened. Keep in mind that a terrified cat can be a danger to you—in that moment, at least.

Alternatively, a threatened or aggressive cat in fight-or-flight mode will puff up the hair on their tail to make themselves appear larger and more formidable. This is especially true if they feel trapped. Fear can easily turn to violence as self-defense, so back off from any of these signs, indoors or out. You should not approach a cat under these circumstances.

When your patio prowler is sitting or lying down, you'll frequently see his tail wrapped around his body for protection. If you're trying to get to know this new backyard tenant, pick a spot several feet away and sit down. In the animal world, size matters, so the smaller you are, the less threatening you appear. It also allows him to sniff you from afar and, over time, realize your presence is harmless. If you're offering food, start by doing it from a safe distance of at least a couple of yards.

When his tail is flicking back and forth, it means the cat's nervous system has been triggered. If you've ever driven a stick shift, you can think of the tail like the tachometer on your car's dashboard telling you when the engine is revving too fast and you need to switch gears. Our cats' tails give us a similar reading on their energy level. It's like someone tapping their fingers while sitting at a desk. The speed of the tapping indicates how tense they are.

House cats also exhibit this tail coding. You've probably seen your family furball's tail twitching when she's watching a bird through the window or stalking a toy in your living room. Once the tail starts swishing faster, particularly when the base of the tail is engaged and not just the tip, be careful; your feline friend is agitated. The faster the tail moves, the higher the likelihood she will pounce on the toy or attack the prey—or the human who has invaded her space.

This feature holds true whether it's a domesticated or a feral cat. Ever notice how playing with your cat can reach a threshold where they suddenly start to bite and use their claws? They're *overstimulated*. If you read the "tell-tale" signs, you can learn to stop before their frolic becomes your doctor's office visit.

House cats use their tails to display happy, confident, or affectionate feelings by holding them straight up or in the shape of a question mark. A community cat who raises his tail to you is most likely a stray who once used this sign with his humans. Feel honored, as this indicates the cat feels relatively secure around you. That does *not* mean you should walk right up and start petting him. Again, always let the cat come to you. But if you do gain his trust enough for him to sidle up close, he may even wrap his tail around your leg in the feline version of a hug.

The cats you care for in your home should be feeling self-assured most of the time and have no need to tuck their tails. If your kitty is habitually exhibiting fear responses, take it seriously and look for what is worrying him. Has something changed in the environment, like a strange visitor, a new pet, or a toddler? Are you having the bathroom remodeled? If it's a temporary situation, your cat will probably hide for the short duration, but if it's a circumstantial change, consider how you can adapt your home to provide a more secure setting. Maybe putting up shelves or adding a cat tree to allow your little fluffball to climb high to safety and still feel part of the household. I wish I had known to do that for Zilly, who was incessantly bullied by my Golden Retriever.

If the tail is glued to his belly, it suggests your cat is terrified of something that already has or will imminently happen, like another pet he's had an altercation with. Try to evaluate all possibilities, and if you can't resolve it, consider contacting a cat behavior expert like Dr. Geller.

Remember to always consult your vet if there's no convincing reason for a behavioral change.

Ears. Ears tell their own tale. Each ear can swivel independently 180 degrees, searching for sounds to alert the cat to her environment. Straight-up ears mean relaxation, confidence, or curiosity. If a cat is enjoying you stroking her, her ears will confirm that. If they're pointing forward, she's focused on something and perhaps about to pounce.

Held horizontally in the shape we call "airplane ears" means the cat is nervous and unsure. And you probably intuitively know that when the ears are pinned back against her head, it denotes the highest defensive posture, used when the cat is afraid or about to become aggressive. They look pretty terrifying like that, but in fact, it's the cat's way of protecting these sensitive organs.

Feral cats generally flatten their ears around humans, either airplane style or pulled all the way back, unless they have come to feel secure in your presence.

 **Posture.** Posture is critical in your interpretation of the cat's mood. Hunkered down means scared, back arched to make themselves appear larger is aggressive, and sitting calmly in a "loaf" position with paws tucked beneath them shows contentment. Remember that in the animal world, fear can rapidly turn to aggression, so never approach a frightened animal without good reason (and if you *must*, be sure to protect yourself).

Hair. When a cat is poised to attack, their fur will be straight up as if charged with static electricity. It makes them look bigger than they actually are and is intended to scare away would-be combatants. Combined with an arched back, it creates the notorious Halloween meme. This strategy is used by numerous mammals in the animal kingdom.

Head bunting. Also known as headbutting. If a cat head bunts you, well, you've pretty much won them over.

Kneading. A cat who "makes biscuits" on a part of your body is offering you the highest affection. Kittens instinctively knead their mothers' bellies to stimulate milk production, and that comforting practice may persist into adulthood. Some cats habitually perform this pastime on their favorite humans when feeling happy and relaxed. It indicates warm feelings, attachment, and trust, while also depositing their scent and claiming that person as their property.

Jackson Galaxy has several great YouTube videos explaining how tails and ears provide valuable information about our feline companions.[13]

VOCALIZATIONS

Our feline friends use their voices to communicate just as we do, and like everything else kittens learn, their mothers are their teachers. As a newborn, mewing gets mama's attention, and as adults, a homed cat gets our attention with a meow.

Even though cats don't meow to each other past kittenhood, they recognize that humans speak to one another, so our socialized little moggies have taken the trouble to expand their lexicon in order to talk with us, even by meowing in different notes. Which is kind of a big compliment, in my opinion. Or perhaps they see us as parental surrogates and are merely using what worked for them as babies, but the more we answer them, the more we reinforce the behavior. Cats can't formulate the syllables we do nor do they have our vocabulary, so it's up to us to learn the language they *can* speak so we're able to respond appropriately. Have you ever noticed that your kitty's meows change in different contexts?

My senior cat is fifteen, and I'm embarrassed to say that it's only been in the last few years that I started to interpret the pitch of her voice. SammieKat will meow when she's about to or has just pooped in the litter box. I used to hear her call from the other room and wonder what was wrong. Nothing. She was just telling me her box was dirty and I should clean it. Lately, I've noticed she meows when she's going to drink water—in a different tone. I still don't know what action she wants me to take for that, as the dish is full—until she spills half on the floor. I'd swear sometimes she washes her paws in it, so maybe she wants the bowl freshened. Since I give her bottled water twice a day, I wish I could convince her to bathe her paws *before* I change the bowl.

Some senior cats meow more as they age, which can be an indication of cognitive decline, or feline cognitive dysfunction. In this feline version of Alzheimer's, older cats can get confused and insecure in the dark or after a certain time of day and exhibit signs akin to "sundowning" in humans with dementia. If your cat is going through this, it's vitally important that you do not scold her if she can't find her litter box or is up yowling at night. She needs solace. Sometimes just leaving a night light on will help. And, of course, as with any behavioral change, you should have her evaluated by her vet to make sure there's nothing systemically wrong.

Even though only our leonine pets meow, in the wild, they have a large portfolio of articulations all their own. They range from hissing to growling, snarling, chirping, trilling, and I'll even throw purring in there, since it's achieved by oscillation of the glottis, the space between the vocal cords. The frequency and volume of purring vary with the cat's intention. By the way, a lion's equivalent to a purr is a roar. The hyoid bones in their necks are not fully ossified, or hardened, so the vibration sounds different. That might qualify as one deterrent to keeping a lion as a pet.

Cats are said to be able to produce a hundred different inflections, and some of that is due to their ability to change the pitch of their voice the way we do when we sing a melody, but each conveys a different message, and each utterance has a meaning.

Some of these are witnessed more indoors, like cats meowing to their human caregivers, and some are (hopefully) reserved for outdoor behavior, like a caterwaul or scream. Even within this list, depending on their upbringing, environment, and personalities, the meanings of your cat's speech may differ somewhat and should be taken in context.

Here are some cat vocalizations, in alphabetical order:

Caterwaul: A loud mating call from female cats in heat. Once spayed, they will not express this.

Chatter: Rapid clicking made when observing prey, indicating excitement or frustration.

Chirp: A short, staccato sound, almost like a bird, which is often made when a cat is watching avians or other quarry perched on your fence outside. It usually signals excitement and is similar to a chatter.

Growl: A throaty sound and a warning to back away, ordinarily accompanied by defensive body posturing.

Grunt: A short, low noise that can indicate either contentment or effort.

Hiss: An onomatopoeia; a word that sounds like its name. It's an early admonition presaging the attack mode that may follow. It signals fear, discomfort, aggression, or just "Get away from me." Have you ever hissed back to give a clear message to stop a certain behavior? It will be understood… although not necessarily *obeyed*.

Meow: A somewhat musical communication in a variety of notes, from alto to soprano. It's solely directed at people and generally means your cat wants something. It's used to request food, attention, or merely to say hello when their favorite human comes home.

Mew: A shorter, high-pitched meow that only kittens use to call their mothers.

Moan: A long, low-pitched sound of agitation or pain.

Mutter: Soft, muffled sounds conveying displeasure.

Purr: A soft, rhythmic, vibratory noise that often indicates contentment and affection. Cats don't just purr to humans; they purr to their kittens, to each other, and for themselves if they're stressed or in pain.

Purring is a remarkable process. It occurs at a frequency of 25 to 100 Hz, or vibrations per second, but the volume and frequency can change as the cat's purpose changes. Sometimes our cuddly companion is purring *at* us, telling us they're happy snuggled in our laps, and sometimes they purr as they circle our legs at feeding time, nudging us to hasten the process. But cats also purr to themselves to soothe their own stress or pain or to heal from an injury. Studies have shown that purring stimulates tissue regeneration and bone regrowth and helps them recoup.[14] See Chapter 7 for an amazing array of healthy perks we humans receive from our cat's purring.

Scream: A loud, hair-raising screech heard during fights or mating.

Silent meow: As you'd expect, a meow that does not produce sound. A gentler meow.

Snarl: An angry, threatening noise that may immediately precede aggression.

Spit: Accompanies a particularly fierce hiss, and sounds louder due to the intensity of forced exhalation. It does not generally expel saliva like our spit does.

Trill: A cross between a meow and a purr, it's higher pitched and sounds a little like a rolled *R* in Spanish. More common in females because mother cats use it to tell their kittens to follow them. When used with humans, it usually denotes affection or greeting.

Yelp: A sudden, reactive sound that resembles a shriek, heard when scared or injured. You can also yelp at your house cat if he scratches or hurts you, and he will understand. I've used this to train my cats not to bite during play.

Yowl: A loud, protracted vocalization denoting distress, confusion, or pain. Sometimes older cats with dementia will vocalize like this.

Among these categories, there can still be diversity. For example, my SammieKat will hiss at different intensities. I've learned to distinguish when her hiss has no venom in it, and it's just her way of saying, "Don't bother me now, I'm not in the mood." She hisses at strangers more forcefully, and if she sees a neighborhood stray through the patio door, the amplification is way up and may be accompanied by a spit. She's undoubtedly telling the intruder, "Back off! This is my turf, and I'm prepared to defend it."

Many of the sounds listed above can be tailored to a given key, much as you can sing a song in the key of C major or D flat. Higher pitches tend to indicate friendship or supplication and lower pitches are more characteristic of fear and aggression.

WHISKERS AT WORK

Not only are whiskers vital sensory organs, but they also communicate emotions. Happy or curious cats elevate the whiskers on their brows, giving them that wide-eyed, irresistibly lovable expression.

When the muzzle whiskers are relaxed, it means your cat is content and her whiskers are taking a break. She'll point them forward when she's curious or generally on alert, since these delicate tendrils access an enormous amount of information about the environment.

If they're pulled backward, however, your kitty is feeling uncertain or fearful, because, in her mind at least, flattening them against her face makes her appear smaller. But besides pulling her muzzle taut, she may also flair her whiskers and direct them forward toward the threat to gather details about her situation.[15] See more about whiskers in Chapter 9, titled "Fun Facts About Cats."

By understanding what the cats in your neighborhood are "saying," you can better meet their needs, and you'll be better equipped to know whether that Tom who keeps looking in your door before and after you feed him is a candidate for coming inside. It can also help you bond even more closely with your house pets.

The bottom line, however, is never try to pick up a strange cat unless they've given you ample reason to believe they welcome your handling them. If they circle your legs, purr, hold their tails high, make eye contact, and eat treats out of your hand, you *may* be okay, but it's not guaranteed. Take it slow. We never know what trauma these animals have survived and what will trigger their survival instinct.

I still can't pick Midnight up to cuddle, and she's been living in "retirement" in my house since August 2021. She lies next to me when I sit on the floor, rests her head on my thigh and looks up with adoring eyes, purrs constantly, eats out of my hand, and loves when I brush her. But she panics if I try to take her in my hands, and although she may not intend to hurt me, her flight response comes with very sharp claws. (As you may imagine, I haven't been able to clip her claws, either.)

CAN YOU/SHOULD YOU BRING ANY CAT INDOORS?

Despite observing their behavior, it's not possible to categorize a cat by saying she's socialized or unsocialized. It's a matter of degree, and that level may change over time. A totally unsocialized, purely feral cat will probably not make themselves visible to you at all, whereas a lost but friendly house cat may come right up to you for help. Most cats will be somewhere in between.

This is not to say you shouldn't adopt a community cat. Strays may need you even more than the cat at the shelter or the feral colony members who have one another to rely on for protection.

If you've made friends with a free-roaming cat and want to bring them inside, consider other animals in your house. Remember, that mouser who's been braving the elements may have picked up something that wouldn't hurt you, but could put your other pets at risk. If you've ever adopted from a shelter, you may recall them telling you to isolate the newcomer for a couple of weeks to make sure they're not carrying anything contagious to your other animals. Your new buddy needs to be checked out by a vet first.

Once you know the cat is healthy, it's still unwise to let your new friend casually walk in and mingle with your house cat. There are recommended ways to help cats meet each other slowly in a controlled environment. If they get off on the wrong paw, those bad memories can make it exceptionally challenging to form positive relationships. There will be more on this in Chapter 5.

Even ferals may be adoptable, but it will take a lot of time and patience on your part, and you'll both need a good reason to enter the process. For instance, John DeBacker rescued a feral who'd become listless and appeared ill. After being trapped and brought to a vet, he was diagnosed with hyperthyroidism. The cat needed daily medication for the rest of his life, making it unreasonable to return him to his colony. Fortunately, the person who'd been feeding the clowder was willing to take him home and socialize him slowly while putting medicine in his food every day.

An important caveat to this success story is that another loving philanthropist, who'd been providing for a neighboring colony, was willing to pay the vet bill. The cost of caring for community cats is high, even with many veterinarians and some town shelters pitching in by offering discounts.

The bottom line is that if a cat is sick or injured and needs medical care, or if your colony is growing exponentially and should be entered into a TNR program—or even if you've just formed a bond and want to bring the little guy inside—someone is going to have to trap him.

- Try a fun exercise: Study your indoor and outdoor cats and practice decoding the messages they're sending with their tails.

CHAPTER 4
TO CATCH A CAT

HOW DO you *safely* trap a cat?

Remember, cats are not only perfect predators, skilled fighters with razor-sharp claws and teeth, but also prey animals with all the survival instincts that come with that. Even if you've made friends, they will undoubtedly interpret your attempt to cage them as a violation. Wouldn't you?

So, what's the first step?

Don't do what I did! I assumed that because Midnight let me pet her, purred at me, and ate treats out of my hand outside my front door, she would accept my picking her up and putting her into a carrier. At least as well as my other cats had. As I prepared to grasp her, I told myself, "You have *one* chance at this." She had been ignoring the open kennel, so I thought I was good, and I felt very intentional about getting her in there.

If you know anything about cats, indoors or out, you're laughing while reading this. It's okay. In retrospect, it was pretty foolish.

As you might imagine, that first attempt to collect Midnight did not go as planned. Never have I seen a cat jump so high—at least six feet. To make matters worse, it was summer, and like an idiot, I was wearing socks but no shoes, so when she launched herself into the air, one paw used the top of my foot to push off. She was oblivious to this, I'm sure, but she left three deep red lines from my toes halfway to my ankle. After two weeks of increasing inflammation, I finally realized that they weren't going away with topical antibiotics and I needed to start oral medicine. The marks finally faded and the infection cleared, but the scars remained for nearly a year.

Following that blunder, she avoided my house for days. Of course. In her mind, it was now labeled DANGER ZONE. I removed the carrier and walked the backyards of my neighborhood calling her name, and worrying she would never return. But hunger must've gotten the best of her, because she finally scouted the area and tentatively approached the food bowl. This time, she would no longer eat if I was within three yards.

All that progress, lost.

That's when I knew I needed help. I turned to my dear friend Marge and learned about trapping.

SNAP TRAPS, AKA HUMANE BOX TRAPS

My hope with this book is to convince some of my readers that trapping is not hard and does not demand a degree in zoology. It *does* require that you learn to do it safely and properly so you don't spook the cat and they don't escape to shred your skin like a cheese grater. You'll find numerous free videos on how to use traps, and I recommend you watch one before you attempt to get your prize. Just go to YouTube and search for "how to trap a cat." (There's a reason they call it YouTube University.)

Besides that, many humane traps for purchase have a short video clip on their online detail page demonstrating the process, so even if you don't buy one, you can still watch how it's done.

If you want to go the extra mile, there are even certification classes, both virtual and in person, depending on where you live, that teach you everything you need to know to be a compassionate and successful trapper. Attendees usually get a list of free or discounted spay/neuter services and other support networks, but you can also find these opportunities in your area with an internet search.

For example, several town shelters on Long Island provide vouchers that you can take to a low-cost vet for the TNR procedure, so your out-of-pocket cost is trivial. Wherever you live, check your local listings to see what is available near you.

But please note: It is *not* necessary to be certified to perform TNR on a cat in your neighborhood *or* to qualify for a subsidy.

The trapping mechanism is fairly simple, but make sure you choose sturdy, well-constructed equipment. Some models are fairly inexpensive, but you might get what you pay for. Look for the options with plenty of positive reviews, and please, *read* the reviews. You need something easy to use—for both you and the cat—that will stand up to the escape antics that invariably follow the first moments inside. Once caught, throwing a towel or blanket over the trap so the cat cannot see out tends to calm them down.

However, you may not need to buy one at all. Many shelters and rescues will loan one to you if you give them a security deposit. Once you've captured and delivered the cat and brought the trap back to the shelter, they'll return your money. When you borrow a trap this way, ask for explicit instructions on how to use it if they don't spontaneously provide that information.

Place the cage near where the cat is used to feeding. The food goes at the far end beyond the trip plate, but some designs have doors on both sides so you don't have to slide the bait in like pizza into a hot oven. The front gate is left open, but to get to the tasty meal, the animal has to step on the metal panel. Their weight triggers the device and closes the gate.

A side note is that raccoons will often be tempted by the food you leave out. Since they are primarily nocturnal creatures, it's advised that if you haven't caught your kitty by nightfall, close up shop and try again with fresh food in the morning. Unless you're trying to catch a raccoon, that is.

Remember that if you get it wrong (or if the cat has previous experience with traps), she may not be fooled by the food at the end of the short tunnel next time, and will never go anywhere near the contraption, no matter how ravenous she is. The survival instinct will overpower any hunger she may be experiencing.

So it was with Midnight. That story continues below.

For the merely reluctant visitor, you can start by tying the trap door open so it cannot be tripped by the plate mechanism. Set the food down outside the cage and a foot or two away, gradually moving it closer with each feed, until you're leaving it just inside. As days go by, keep pushing the flavorsome fare farther back, until the cat is feeling confident walking all the way in to get her grub.

Then, untie the door and set the trap.

Do *not* start this process until you have a secure plan in place, which includes an appointment with a vet and a strategy for where you're going to keep the cat after treatment. Whether the little scruffball is sick, injured, or just getting neutered, she will need a secure place to recover postoperatively or for rest and continued medication. Females need about three days to convalesce after being spayed, but males are usually good to go in twenty-four hours. You may not yet know if it's a girl or a boy, so prepare for either.

Don't ever trap a cat first and then try to figure out what you're going to do with her later.

A trap divider, or fork, is a useful tool that can facilitate care during recovery. By inserting it through the cage from the side, you can isolate the cat away from the gate so you can clean the space and replace food safely without being scratched or bitten.

After my fiasco with Midnight, my friend Marge loaned me a

humane trap and showed me how to use it, but alas, my kitty was not to be fooled. Not only did she remember my doltish attempt to get her in a carrier, but her tipped ear—the universal sign that she was part of the TNR program—signaled that she'd obviously been trapped before. Suddenly, she preferred to find her own meals—or starve.

It was the dog days of summer when I decided to bring her in. Over the months, I had observed that she was a drooly cat. This made sense when I later learned she's missing twenty teeth. But that August, it was in the 90s every day, and my little Tuxedo was becoming lethargic and dehydrated. No more drooling, minimal activity, and on top of that misery, she was plagued by ear mites.

After failing with the snap trap, I gave it back to Marge and again put food and water out for my little friend. She would not touch the water, so I chose canned food with the most gravy I could find. The moisture in the food might have been enough, except she was too skittish, or maybe too weak, to eat much.

Then one day, she lay under my car, and although she was breathing, she didn't so much as twitch an ear when I walked up and spoke to her. I called my friend Marge again.

DROP TRAPS

In preparation for capture, I contacted my vet's office, described the problem, and solicited their agreement to see Midnight that day *if* I could catch her. Then I set up a new litter box in the extra bathroom upstairs.

Marge brought a new apparatus: a drop trap. Like the other one, it was also a wire cage, although much larger and square-shaped instead of a rectangle, but this one had no bottom. She raised it off the ground at a 60-degree angle, supporting the

end by a metal bar. This meant the area immediately surrounding the food was clear. Despite the odd sort of ceiling, most of the cage wasn't touching the ground, and was able to successfully masquerade as a safe place to eat.

And then I learned what it means to be a trapper. The bottom of the support rod was attached to a string that Marge ran along the driveway to behind my car, where she could sit out of sight. And we waited.

If you are trapping in a wooded area, you may be able to camouflage your snare with leaves or by placing objects around it to make it blend into the environment—just take care not to obstruct the closing mechanism. I didn't have that option; Midnight was used to eating on my front porch.

I don't remember how long it took. A half hour? An hour? Quiet as a cat stalking a mouse, my friend sat there and barely moved. I was inside the house at a window with a clear view of the trap and the food. (I definitely had the more comfortable job.) Finally, the Tuxedo appeared. She stopped repeatedly to scratch furiously at her ears, then gazed appraisingly at the food under the weird-looking metal thing. It kind of looked like a trap, but... not quite.

Finally, she stepped inside and started to dine, and I texted Marge to pull the string. When the trap came down, Midnight's frenzied movements caused the whole cage to slide along the pavement, and since there is no floor to these traps, she could have conceivably broken free by bouncing against the chamber until it lifted a few inches. Quickly, the veteran trapper and I stabilized the frame and threw a cloth over the top.

Note: Always set up your drop trap on a level field, be close enough to arrive before the cat's frantic movements allow escape, and use a blanket or sheet to cover it and calm the cat.

Once Midnight quieted, Marge brought a transfer cage that attached to the side of the drop trap, offering the only exit. Thankfully, Midnight walked into it, and Marge closed the door. That accessory cage brought my little prowler to the veterinarian.

There's a funny story with that.

With the doors to the exam room closed, the vet tech brought out a scale and started opening the cage.

"Be careful," I said. "She's a *stray* cat, she's going to try to make a break for it."

But my warning was too late.

As resourceful and petrified cats are known to do, once she smelled freedom, Midnight took flight. No matter that it was a small space, she bounced off the table onto the *wall*, clinging to the upper rim of a framed diploma, and from there vaulted to the *top* of supply cabinets that extended nearly to the drop ceiling on which she bumped her head. One of the plates moved a few inches, but fortunately fell back in place.

And there she sat. Eight feet high and totally out of our reach.

The rattled technician opened the door a crack and called out, "Loose cat. Need some help in here."

Another staff member came in with bite-proof gloves and a small ladder. She climbed up and managed to snag my little mouser and bring her back to the exam table, where she thereafter cooperated—for the most part.

I had never seen such thick mitts before. Irrefutably, they're an essential tool for anyone working with unpredictable cats, but don't try to find your car keys with these on. They afford virtually no manual dexterity. About the only thing they're good for, as far as I could tell, is catching or restraining an animal who may try to bite or claw you. Too bad we can't make gloves out of mithril, like Frodo's impenetrable shirt in *The Lord of the Rings*.

If you don't yet know, you may get a sense of where your cat is on the spectrum of stray by looking at their behavior in the trap. Most ferals will slink to the back of the crate and stay there. Previously socialized cats will exhibit the same fear behavior initially, but are more likely to relax after a day or two and move forward in the cage. They may even come sniff your fingers at the front gate. Ferals never do this.

CAMERAS

Felines are an ingenious species, and they can detect your stalking maneuvers. If they sense a human near the trap you've left, the enticement of food becomes secondary to their survival instinct. In order to pull off a successful trapping, you have to be out of sight, out of sound—and out of smell.

The beauty of the snap trap over the drop trap is that you can set it and leave it to do its work. You can even conceal it in some cases. But suppose you're trying to trap a cat a mile from home or one who doesn't seem to be in a hurry to visit? Setting cameras in a building or a shed with the ability to monitor activity from your phone is an excellent solution. Some systems have motion detectors that will send you an alert once the trap is triggered. Then you can collect the little mouser without having had to sit outside until she made an appearance.

CATCH POLE NETS

Okay, but what if you need to catch that cat *now*, and there's no time to wait for it to mosey into a cage looking for food? Perhaps it's fallen into a ditch or it's in the middle of traffic, too scared to even think about food? See John DeBacker's story titled "Merry," in Chapter 6.

That's where a catch pole net comes in, but realize that the kitty is going to be just as frightened by the net as it is of its current circumstances. Maybe more so. And this technique takes skill beyond the setup of a cage.

The potential for injury to both animal and human is much greater here, and I do *not* recommend you try this without proper training and guidance. Again, many of these have video instructions on their detail page, but you may need more direction than that.

Catch poles exist in varying net sizes. You'll want a fine mesh that doesn't allow the cat's paws to poke through. She is undoubtedly going to try to escape, and her paws can get caught in the holes and twist. The last thing you want is to rescue the kitten from the highway but leave her with a broken leg. In addition, no matter the size of the net, you might get clawed yourself.

Some nets have zippers at the bottom to allow you to release your prize directly into a carrier. While you should be able to grab the cat by the scruff through the net like its mother used to do, this is not recommended unless absolutely necessary. Scruffing an adult cat can be painful, cause fear and anxiety, and may trigger a potentially aggressive reaction. If used in anything other than a dire emergency, it's also likely to erode any trust the cat will have in humans going forward. Use it only as a last resort.

CATCHING A COMMUNITY CAT WITH YOUR HANDS

This is *not* recommended. The exception would be if the cat is so injured as to be unable to move on their own. Even if they appear listless, your hands on a feral may activate a fight-or-flight response that overpowers their infirmity, and they could lash out.

It's best if you call for help from a rescue, animal control, or someone like John DeBacker, who makes it his business to deal with cats in severely compromised situations.

If you have no other options and are set on retrieving the cat, use thick, heavy gloves—the ones that are bite-proof are the best choice, although they afford little maneuvering power. If you don't have those, improvise. In addition, bring a towel to wrap around the wounded cat and encase their paws. Have a carrier nearby when you reach for her so that you can quickly deposit the animal in the kennel and transport them directly to a veterinary hospital.

Again, scruffing is a last-ditch resort and only for short distances.

This is where you gently but firmly grasp the fur on the back of the neck without pinching, much like a mama cat carries her babies. As you lift the kitty, immediately support her hind legs (avoiding the claws) and deliver her quickly to safety.

But keep in mind, you are *not* a mama cat. The resultant immobility that looks like a calming effect is likely a state of shock, fear, and helplessness. Sometimes the cat will manage to squirm and twist around to scratch you, which may injure you both. In addition, depending on what happened to the cat to require rescue, you might harm her further.

Not all cats can be deftly scruffed, either. Kittens are easier than adult cats, but it ultimately depends on how loose their skin is, which can vary by breed, weight, and overall muscle tone. If there is no other alternative, make scruffing as brief as possible. Reserve this practice for getting a cat out of danger, and do not use this at home on your indoor cats or newbie strays you're trying to socialize. They will associate human handling with trauma, and it could set you back so that the cat won't be willing to trust you again.

In general, never try to pick up a feral cat at all.

Even after all these years, Midnight still jumps and runs away if I put two hands on her at once. I'm trying to desensitize her by brushing her with one hand while stroking her cheek with the other, but it's taken forever to get this far—and she was never even a true feral. After her last trip to the vet, she marched downstairs to SammieKat's "territory," squeezed herself into a kitty condo, and would not come out for food or the litter box for forty-eight hours. My little baby was shell-shocked.

NO KIT-NAPPING!

While kit napping kittens is not a federal offence, you're doing harm if you take them from their mama. Kittens need their mothers for the first six to eight weeks of life. After the first couple of days, it's not unusual for the molly to leave her litter for short periods of time to search for food or safer lodgings. Don't mistake this for abandonment. By "rescuing" immature babies, you are endangering their lives, since they must now be bottle fed *every* meal and will not have the sound tutelage of their most important teacher. Not to mention—you're breaking the mama's heart.

That's not to say you should leave kittens to die. Observe the nest to make sure the mother does come back. If you see one lone kitten, the mom may be in the process of moving her children. She can only carry one at a time, so someone is going to be first or last.

The younger the kittens, the more they need their mother's warmth for survival, and the less time the mother will stay away. Newborns are more at risk from hypothermia than from starvation. If the kittens appear cold, sick, distressed, or in peril, or if the mother has not come back in 24 hours, then you may need to retrieve the litter.[16]

Keep in mind that if you take a kitten who is less than four weeks old, they will need to be bottle-fed, which requires additional skills. If you see deserted kittens too young to eat solid food, get in touch with your veterinarian or local shelter for advice.

8 STEPS TO TRAP A CAT

1. Identify *who* and *why* you want to trap.
2. Acquire the equipment you'll need: type of trap, tasty meals, trap divider, and a smart camera that alerts your phone when motion is detected.
3. Determine the cat's customary feeding area and start providing food on a regular schedule.
4. Prepare a cozy place to keep the cat (or cats) before and after seeing the vet.
5. Make an appointment with a veterinarian.
6. Set up transportation to the clinic.
7. Begin moving the food into the trap and set it.

8. Postoperatively, bring the patient back to the comfort zone you've prepared or to a previously arranged foster home to recuperate.

- It is *not* necessary to be certified in order to perform TNR on a cat in your neighborhood.

CHAPTER 5
CAT'S OUT OF THE BAG

FROM BUSHES TO CUSHIONS

SO, let's say you've got a clean bill of health from the vet's office and you now have a new set of whiskers in your home. A community cat somewhere on the spectrum of socialization, from fearful feral, wholly unaccustomed to humans, to a stray who was abandoned a week ago and is frightened, confused, and grieving. (Yes, cats mourn the loss of their families.) All can exhibit the same behaviors when they feel threatened, so it's sometimes hard to determine where on the scale your little feline falls.

Whether or not there is already a resident pet in your home, it's

best to put the newcomer into a "sanctuary room," someplace they can feel secure in their new surroundings, away from people and other animals. Make sure it's cat-proof, meaning it does not contain anything dangerous or fragile, and, if you can, block off access to the space behind the couch or under the bed. Your new occupant needs places to hide, for sure, but you don't want him to be out of your reach should you need to get to him. Add a little kitty condo or a cardboard box instead. Place food, water, and a litter box inside the room, and keep the door closed. This will help your newcomer relax.

Frightened cats tend to slink under furniture, but once they become more confident, they'll often prefer to take refuge on high ground. Scratching is a natural instinct that reduces stress, marks territory by depositing pheromones, and of course, keeps their claws ready for hunting and self-defense.

You cannot keep your cat from scratching, but you can redirect this behavior.

A cat tower can address all of these needs and is an excellent addition to your safe room. Many have hidey-holes and a platform on top from which they can survey the world, and most come equipped with a scratching post. The sisal or rope-covered styles most closely resemble the outdoors and are usually attractive to your tenant. Plus, climbing is good exercise, and if the kitty tree is near a window, it can provide hours of cat TV.

GETTING TO KNOW YOUR CAT

After you've set up Tigger's new room, start spending time in there. Even if there's little to no interaction initially, acclimating the cat to your presence is the first step. Sit quietly on the floor a few feet away and speak softly. If he runs from you, ignore him and surf the web on your tablet or phone. Just let the little critter get used to your smell and having you nearby. Remember to wait for the cat to invite you into his space.

Just like each human has a distinct personality and a unique soul, no cat is like another. They have different tastes, different personalities, and different needs. In order to understand *this* cat's behavior, you must take the time to get to know your furry friend. Your present kitty will *not* be the same as your last one. The good news is that there are common communication strategies.

Start by observing. What scares them and what do they feel comfortable with? Try to put yourself in their paws and look at the world through their eyes. Standing maybe a foot tall, surrounded by strange sights and smells, no familiar hiding places, and needing to strategize. They're deciding what they can and cannot trust.

Their body language will tell you a lot. All those signs we talked about when evaluating a cat's mood outside apply equally well inside. Ultimately, we hope to see more of the happy signals in our homes, those behaviors that mean the cat feels safe and secure, and ultimately, to display affection.

After the little mouser has relaxed enough to sit in the loaf position, with tail quiet or only minimal twitching, try looking at him from a few feet away. In the animal kingdom at large, eye contact may precede hostility, so your new adoptee may look away if you gaze at him. This simply means he does not want to engage, and can be a positive sign because he isn't preparing to run or fight.

Once you've connected with him visually, soften your eyes the way you would with someone you love, and blink. Let your eyes stay closed for a half to a full second. If he blinks back, celebrate! But—quietly. No sudden or loud movements at this stage. It means he trusts you enough to close his eyes and make himself vulnerable. The feline blink is a universal sign of goodwill and eventually, of affection.

In the same vein, a cat who sits with his back to you is also feeling relatively secure, trusting that you won't ambush him when he's not looking.

Try to offer a treat and see if the little munchkin will come get it. Always let the cat approach you, and hold your hand low so it's not perceived as a threat, never above his head. If he's not ready to eat from your fingers, place it between you, and maybe he'll edge closer. Take things at the cat's pace.

When your new arrival allows you to touch him, continue to follow his cues. However, if he rolls over and shows you his belly, do *not* take this bait! Stroke his head instead. A common mistake cat parents make is to interpret this submissive posture as an invitation to pet his tummy—an act that may well precipitate an unwanted response.

Cats look vulnerable with their undersides exposed, but in fact, it frees up all four paws to grab their prey and all four sets of claws to tear that prey to pieces. It's partly reflexive, so beware. That's not to say you can never give your kitty a belly rub, but proceed with caution.

Similarly to humans, cats like routine. If you can establish regular feeding and visitation times, it will help him adjust more quickly. Knowing what to expect and when provides a measure of security.

Once Tigger has become comfortable in his sanctuary room and is exploring his surroundings, and if there are no other pets in the house, you can open the door and let him venture out to investigate the rest of your home.

If he hasn't been around humans for a long time or was born outside, the socialization process will take a while. Be patient. Some cats will warm up to their human family relatively quickly, and others may take weeks or even months. It's up to the cat. Kittens bond with us more quickly than adults do.

Between two and seven weeks old is considered to be the critical window during which it's easiest to socialize a baby cat, but it can extend to fourteen weeks. The more the kitten is handled during that time, the more readily they will accept us as caregivers later in life. That said, if you're willing to be patient, even older cats may still adapt to us humans, especially if they understand they've been rescued from danger. However, in general, the older the cat and the less prior contact with people they've had, the more challenging it will be. Yet, some true ferals have become mush after escaping dire circumstances when they're matched with the right person.

This is all assuming that the cat needs to be indoors. In many cases, a feral is happy and healthy remaining outside with shelter and regular feedings. Every situation is different.

THE POWER OF PLAY

Bonding is easier when there is common ground, and just as a game of pickleball can be a fairly neutral first date between friends, playing with our whiskered wonders affords us a great opportunity to get to know each other.

Dr. Rachel Geller places a lot of emphasis on the importance of play and what that activity means to a feline. When I read her suggestions, it was an aha moment for me. I wish I'd known this years ago—or rather, my *cats* wish I'd known it.

For us, play means leaving work behind, but for cats, play should simulate the hunt. For them, the experience of being an accomplished predator is like getting an A on your chemistry test. Geller believes that our mousers can suspend the reality of a stuffed toy on a string and see it as actual prey to be stalked, seized, and consumed. Success in this endeavor creates confidence and joy—especially if there's food to be had at the conclusion. When your companion pet shares this exciting game with you, it just might make you her favorite human.

I have often played with my cats by having them chase an object, but I used to pull it away when they reached it until they were scuttling around the room. In my mind, it was giving them exercise and tapping into their instincts, but I was unwittingly frustrating them after repeated failed attempts. When our expert hunter can attack and, after a whirlwind pursuit, *contain* her prize, she's so much happier. By following that up with a treat, it mirrors what would happen in the wild when she successfully captures her meal and devours it. And just like our triumphs do for us, victory releases feel-good hormones in her brain.

Conversely, laser toys are a poor choice for cat play. Your proud predator's efforts are always thwarted as she pounces—and finds nothing between her paws. The little red dot is not something tangible that can be acquired. When she's unable to achieve her purpose, no matter how hard she tries, she can get agitated, and the last thing you want is an anxious cat. There's another problem with lasers. Unless you're careful to get one labeled as safe for pets, it can damage a cat's eyes if they look directly into the light. For these reasons, they are not recommended.

Wand toys are often the best choice because they keep you at a distance from swatting claws, and the feathered phony at the end of the string can behave more lifelike by scampering about under your direction.

Dr. Geller recommends that you have the toy mimic what live prey would do. A rodent would never run up to a predator to get their attention, it would hide or scurry away and then struggle or play dead if caught. So, think like a mouse when you draw the wand toy across your cat's field of vision, and of course, make it fun by having it "escape" a few times after she tackles it. But eventually, let your cat win, and give a tasty morsel so your puddy can revel in her success.

SammieKat used to jump and spin four feet in the air, chasing a bird on a stick that she occasionally caught with no help from me. I still have those hysterical video recordings. It sometimes took a quarter of an hour for her to tire out.

Many cats also love a good game of hide-and-seek because it simulates ferreting out their quarry. I can always get Sammie to come to me if I lie low and hide behind a wall or piece of furniture, checking on her every few seconds. She crouches down with her pupils dilated and wiggles her whole body (including her tail) until she finally dashes over to where she last saw my face. Although she doesn't actually pounce on me, she struts around after "finding" me as if she's won the queendom.

Sam has always enjoyed playing with a noisy ball or round toy she can kick around, and she'll nudge it into the kitchen or at my feet when she wants attention and then wait for me to pass it back. We play soccer like this until she sends the ball somewhere I can't get to easily. This doesn't quite fit with the sensible advice from our behavior specialist that suggests we have the toy behave like a prey animal. I can only think that, over the years, my cat has learned to accommodate my daft brain, preferring to play together in whatever way my feeble mind can fathom. It astounds me how much compromise cats are capable of when they love their human.

At her mature age of fifteen, Sammie has slowed down a bit, and last fall, she tore her ACL running up the stairs. At least that's what we surmised, short of sedating her to get an MRI of her knee. The lesson here is to tailor the play to your cat's age and abilities. Jumping enthusiastically may not be an option for an older or disabled cat.

And be patient. Play may not be an early activity for your new arrival. It took Midnight *years* before she would pay attention to any toys, whether they were wand toys moving on a string, balls rolling on the floor, or catnip-stuffed mice. It was as if she thought I was nuts to expect her to treat them as authentic. She knew what a bird was, and these were definitely not real.

I'm happy to say that she does play now, albeit only in spurts, and she seems to like the wand toys best.

Once settled in, your new resident needs activity to keep from getting bored, and play will satisfy that. Outside, he had the neighborhood to explore, with all its sights, sounds, smells, and adventures, even though it was not all frolic and fun. The outdoors holds numerous perils that can cause anxiety for cats, so if you can keep them entertained inside, they'll integrate more smoothly.

You can't sit in their sanctuary space all day, every day, but you can leave them toys to amuse themselves with, including puzzle feeders. By putting food in these, your cat has to use his hunting skills to retrieve each morsel, mimicking the act of tracking down prey for his meal. Variations are available for kibble or canned preferences. However, if your buddy is not eating from these toys, of course, replace them with regular cat bowls for feeding.

Adjustment for many cats can be aided by using artificial pheromones that promote contentment. However, see how your resident reacts. Not all will find this comforting. When I brought Midnight home, SammieKat was not on board with my project that involved her sharing her space, and I was advised to try spraying pheromones and putting one of these collars on her. She was absolutely miserable, and it wasn't from having a band around her neck. She wore a collar from kittenhood to shortly after her fourteenth birthday (when she decided she'd had enough). I believe the scent did not agree with her. Even in her sleep, her face looked tense and unhappy, and she improved dramatically when I removed the pheromone collar and put her usual one back on. I don't believe her reaction was representative, since I have heard that it does help many cats adapt.

It's just another example that there's no one size fits all when it comes to facilitating their adjustment.

- For us, play means to leave work behind, but for cats, play should simulate the hunt.

BRINGING TWO CATS TOGETHER

If you're bringing your new adoptee into a house with another cat, it's doubly important to have that sanctuary room set up with a closed door beforehand. I have to say, when I brought Midnight into my home with SammieKat, I did everything wrong. However, in retrospect, it became an enormous teaching moment that, at least in part, gave birth to this book.

I foolishly thought that because SammieKat had insinuated herself into Zilly's personal space as a kitten, she would accept another feline cousin. I forgot that initially, Zilly wanted nothing to do with her, and it was only her fearless persistence, refusing to be rejected, and her tiny size that eventually won him over. A two-pound ball of fluff following an eighteen-pounder around until he finally relented.

I also did not consider that it had been eight years since Zilly left us, and Sammie had gone from little princess to queen of the roost.

But most significantly, I did not account for the fact that cats have distinct personalities, tastes, and preferences, just like humans do, and they prefer to choose their own friends, thank you. Apparently, two adult females are the hardest combination to bring together.

But it's not impossible. First of all, it's vitally important that each cat has their own protected space, with food, water, and a litter box separate from the other cats in the house. These items should be placed in an area where the cat cannot be easily cornered by another pet. The rule of thumb is to have as many boxes as there are cats plus one extra. That way, no one has to chase someone else out of the potty or find an objectionable substitute when they need to do their business.

When making your first introduction, delay the visual connection; don't allow them to see each other. Let the newbie calm down and get comfortable in her sanctuary room while your resident cat acclimates to the idea of another animal in the house. Then, begin feeding or giving treats to both cats on either side of the door at the same time (you may need an assistant for this).

In this way, they can *smell* each other, but cannot see each other. Let them sniff one another from behind the safety of a closed barrier. You can also take a sock, towel, or other piece of clothing and rub it on each animal's fur, then swap it out for the one you rubbed on the sister cat. It will help them get used to each other's scent without looking them in the eyes.

When that's going well, replace the closed door with a see-through baby gate or a screen to protect from any acts of aggression. When they notice each other, reinforce their acknowledgment with a treat tossed behind them to interrupt the interaction while it's still peaceful. Over the course of several days, promote calm, cheerful behavior with parallel play, meals, and treats, gradually moving the toys and tasty morsels closer to the gate.

At some point, they should become curious about each other, or at least neutral, and then you can let them spend limited time together. Do this when they are relatively content after being fed or tuckered out by play, and supervise them.

Be prepared to intervene if they start to fight—but *not* with your hands. Have immediate access to something that makes a loud noise, a towel you can throw on one of them, or a pillow to push them apart. PAWS recommends a squirt bottle.[17]

Caveat: *Never* let your cats fight it out. I'm not sure this even works with human children, but with felines, they will form negative associations that will be very difficult to reprogram.

Some cats bond fairly easily with other cats, while others never do. You may have to settle for a peaceful coexistence. But just because it doesn't happen in the first few

months, doesn't mean it never will. It can take time.

If one cat constantly bullies the other or frequently runs away and hides, please consult a professional. Dr. Rachel Geller offers support for cat guardians, and has helped countless pet families achieve and sustain harmony in the household. She does not charge for her services, although a donation is most welcome if you are able. Her contact information is in the back of this book.

If you already had more than one cat when the newbie arrives, introduce him to each cat individually so that no one gets ganged up on. Only after the new arrival has met everyone should you allow them all to mingle. And again, please supervise this in the beginning.

Happy cats make for happy relationships, so give your kitties plenty of comfy spots and places to retreat to for alone time. Some like to survey their domain from up on high, so installing traversable shelves or purchasing kitty condos can make your feline's day. Others are less secure and prefer to pass their time in a more enclosed, ground-level hidey-hole. A cardboard box might be their favorite. Of course, one cat may prefer each of these options at different times as their mood shifts. The more cats in your home, the more cozy spots you should provide.

- Never let your cats fight it out.

DECLAWING—*DON'T!*

Many people do not realize that declawing your cat doesn't merely remove her claws; it takes *one-third of her toes* with it. It's not a nail excision, but an *amputation*. When you look at your human hand, you'll see that your fingers each have two knuckles dividing them into three bones, each of which is called a phalanx. Cats also have three phalanges per toe (except for their thumbs, or dewclaws), and the declawing procedure detaches the entire last third of their digits. Think how you'd feel with your fingers cut off after the second joint.

In fact, declawing is now illegal in many states, including New

York, Maryland, Virginia, and Washington, DC, as well as in multiple cities across the country. If your cat does not take to a vertical scratching post, you can find a large selection of pads and ground-level scratchers for purchase pretty much anywhere pet supplies are sold.

Sure, a cat without claws won't destroy your favorite armchair, but he also won't be able to defend himself from other pets in the household, and if he gets out, he's cooked. As a cat lover, I have learned to choose my furniture by its fabric. Tighter weaves are less enticing than knits. You can also throw a cover over your sofa while you're training your cat to use the scratch pad instead of the couch.

- You cannot and should not keep your cat from scratching, but you *can* redirect this behavior.

SETTING LIMITS

For the record, it is absolutely possible to train a cat. Animals are most easily tutored when they are both intelligent *and* eager to please. Dogs have been bred for this combination and are known for being trainable. Cats are every bit as smart as dogs, but are generally not nearly as willing to conform. Their independent nature does not include a desire to ingratiate themselves with us humans, so the motivation is not inherently there. However, if you have a relationship with your cat in which he *wants* to make you happy, all things are attainable. The degree to which your reward is enticing is also a factor.

I know what you're going to ask. How do you make your cat want to please you? Start by seeing the world through his eyes. And remember, no one ever owns a cat.

Over the forty-something years I've had feline friends, after a period of settling in, I've never failed to establish a relationship of mutual respect and rules. My policy was simple: If I don't sit on it, you can't sit on it. That applied to counters, tables, beds, sofas, and chairs. I think they appreciated the fairness of that principle. Sure, that's tongue in cheek, but except for a few transgressions, it's worked for the most part.

There were a few exceptions, like Zilly finding his way into a cabinet over a desk. He'd open it and climb in, and it would shut behind him. He could give anyone an adrenaline jolt if they were hard at work when he suddenly nosed through the door and casually jumped down.

But seriously, half the battle with training is having the expectation that the animal will understand and comply. The other part is comradery. Being the regal and eminently dignified souls that cats are, teaching with courtesy and reward will always get you further than punishment (this is probably also true for other species, like puppies and human children). So when your cat exhibits an unwanted behavior, redirect them with firmness and then reward the new activity.

If their unwanted conduct satisfies a need for them, like scratching or stalking, or occupying their mind when they're bored, see how you can provide an alternative that will be equally satisfying yet not destructive.

While nothing is foolproof, once your cat understands that you mean business and that they will be rewarded for following the rules, they're more likely to be accommodating. Just like kids.

You can also employ clicker training, which teaches your cat to associate the click with a treat, and many feline enthusiasts have taught their cats to perform tricks or jump into a carrier when needed. Believe it or not, some particularly precocious  prowlers have even learned to use a human toilet.

- Cats are highly intelligent, emotional creatures who are finicky about who they form social bonds with.

CHAPTER 6
REAL RESCUES BY JOHN DEBACKER

JOHN DEBACKER IS something of an icon in the New York Tri-State area. He regularly monitors Facebook groups that cater to strays and ferals, and I doubt a day goes by when someone hasn't tagged him to help with an emergency rescue. He's been featured on news media outlets such as NBC, USA, Channel 12, and *The Dodo*, and in *Newsday* and *The New York Post*—to name just a few. John has devoted his life to saving cats and has gained significant notoriety by daring to rescue them under hazardous conditions.

Many shelters and local authorities give out his contact information, and he says he's even been called by people out of state and across the country. This accentuates how sad the situation is. Every day, cats find themselves in danger.

Below are a few of his more sensational stories, written in his own voice.

However, please keep in mind this **DISCLAIMER:**

Do **NOT** attempt these feats on your own without support from competent rescue organizations or individuals who are knowledgeable about *both* cat behavior and trapping, *and* whatever environment the cat has found itself in.

In short, **never risk your own life or limb** to get a cat out of jeopardy.

In the interest of protecting the privacy of those loving individuals who assisted John on these undertakings, their names have been withheld and are referred to simply by the first letter of their first name.

OAKLEY

Last fall, a resident in Hempstead awoke to screams coming from a tree, where a tiny kitten was stuck approximately thirty feet high. He was not sure what to do, so he called the Hempstead Animal Shelter in Wantagh for assistance and was given my number.

I was available at the time and arrived shortly after. I sprang into action with a twenty-foot ladder in one hand and a GoPro camera on my head to film everything, as I do for most rescues.

I climbed up holding on to the tree with one hand and carrying cat food in the other. As I approached the top of the ladder, the kitten was still a good ten feet above me, and there were no sturdy branches to step up on.

Unable to go higher, I asked the homeowners if they had a taller ladder, but they did not, so I cracked open the canned food and attempted to coax the kitty down. His cries only got louder.

Then the mewing became frantic. I spread the cat food on the tree, hoping to entice him, and called to the kitten. Suddenly, he jumped—right into my hand! The little guy stopped mewing as soon as I had him. He knew he was safe.

I dropped the food and came down with the kitten in one hand and holding the tree with the other, and transported him to Last

Hope Animal Shelter. He spent a few weeks there before he was brought to a foster home in Levittown. A friend of mine in Bellmore adopted him about a month or two later.

I loved him so much that I visited him frequently and was so excited that he would live close to me.

We named him Oakley. He was only about six weeks old when I saved him. He either chased an animal up the tree or, more likely, another animal chased him up. We looked but never found the mother or the rest of the litter.

Oakley's story was seen on *The Dodo*, a website that publishes a variety of animal-related articles, and was also featured on *Inside Edition*.

MERRY

It was two days before Christmas in 2023, and cold, as usual. The *CAT & KITTEN Fostering & Adoption Network of NJ* is one of several Facebook groups that I monitor, and photos of a cat with a jar stuck over its head were being posted. The area had a large colony of feral cats that caring residents had been feeding for a while.

Multiple rescue attempts had been made, but the terrified little brown Tabby managed to scurry away each time, even with her head jammed into a clumsy container. This went on for a few days, with neighbors, rescue volunteers, and even animal control going to the scene whenever she was spotted. But Merry—as we later named her—slipped past them all. We started to worry that she would not survive.

There was no way she could eat or drink, and even getting a full breath of air must have been difficult. It was a wonder she had the strength to keep running from us, but like so many feral cats, she did not understand we meant to help her. Who knows what other calamities she'd been through in the past to make her wary of humans? It was starting to look hopeless.

Then, on Christmas morning, while I was opening presents with my family in Middlesex, New Jersey, my friend M texted me that she had eyes on the little kitty, who was hiding behind a shed in her neighbor's yard. And she asked, could I come *now*?

I told M not to approach or make any noise. I didn't want the cat to get spooked. I jumped into my car without even telling anyone where I was going. It took thirty minutes to get there, and it felt like the longest half hour of my life. I arrived just as E, another volunteer friend, came on the scene. I grabbed my usual cat-catching gear, which included a catch pole net and a towel to protect myself. Although this little one would not be able to bite me with its head buried in plastic, she could still fight back with her claws.

For all that, I didn't have a definite plan. I was just figuring it out as I went.

I hopped the fence into the yard where the cat was hiding and crept forward stealthily. She stayed pretty still until I got close. When I reached for her, she tried to bolt away, but not before I was able to grab her with one hand. E quickly brought a carrier over, and I dropped her in from the top.

Scared as she was, the kitty calmed down once enclosed in the crate. I reached in gingerly and was able to gently twist the jar off her head. Perhaps that alone gave her some trust in human beings.

M took her home to foster and had her evaluated and treated when 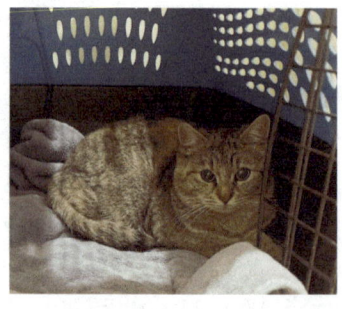 vet offices opened after the holiday. It was a true Christmas miracle. Merry might have sustained neck or throat trauma from the weight of the jar or become dehydrated from lack of water, but she suffered *no* significant injuries.

After a few months, Merry was socialized enough to be adopted into her forever home, where she is still thriving.

Many ferals are never able to adjust and become house cats, but our furry friends are smart. Merry understood that her life had been saved, and she lost her fear of people.

WANDA

In August 2024, I was in Baldwin trying to catch a cat that snuck into someone's garage and had been living there for a week, when my phone started blowing up with an urgent plea for help in Wantagh, a town about thirty minutes away.

When I realized how dire the call was, I immediately packed up and headed straight for the Wantagh Parkway.

While on her way to work, a motorist named K noticed something odd in the center of the highway. She drove by, but looking in her rearview mirror, she realized it was a tiny kitten. The kitten was looking up and watching every passing car drive by, but no one stopped to save her.

As soon as K arrived at work, she made a plea on Facebook for someone to help. I was tagged about it multiple times and saw the post instantly. I left the garage in Baldwin and raced to the scene. I didn't see the kitten on my first pass, but I got off at the next exit to loop around and spotted a tiny Tortie huddled against the center median—too terrified to move.

I pulled off onto the right shoulder and braced myself for a challenging maneuver and called state troopers, who arrived very quickly. Apparently, other drivers had also called 911, so they were already aware of the situation. The officer stopped all traffic in the northbound direction while I performed the difficult rescue.

I approached the kitten slowly, as I've done a thousand times over, but she darted toward traffic. I had so many things racing through my mind, thinking we had just lost her, and she would either hop the barrier and get hit by a passing car—or even climb up inside a stopped vehicle. It was an extremely delicate situation. I had to give a short chase while being careful not to follow directly behind her so she wouldn't think I was pursuing her and run faster. When I caught up to her, I quickly used my net to safely get her off the highway.

After I had the kitten in the net, I ran to my van and transferred her to an empty trap. The cop pulled up next to me to make sure things were going okay and I didn't need help.

Once traffic started to move again, but while still parked on the side of the road, I called around to various rescues, shelters, and fosters. D from Last Hope agreed to take the cat, and we named her Wanda. She was still too young to be adopted, so she stayed at Last Hope, growing and getting socialized. I stopped by almost every day to visit. She was one of my most memorable rescues because of how close things were to going horribly wrong. Each time I saw her, she was friendlier than before.

The original caller filled out an application and adopted Wanda as one of her own.

Her rescue was featured on several news stations, including News 12, CBS, and *Inside Edition*, and it even aired on 1010 WINS radio the following morning.

HOUSE FIRE

In 2024, there was a devastating house fire in Hicksville that left a total of thirty some-odd cats missing, both house cats and ferals that the family was feeding outside. Although I was called as soon as the fire was underway, first responders weren't letting anyone near, even after the blaze was doused, until they determined the cause and whether it was safe to walk around.

When I got there the next day, I searched the perimeter while workers constructed a protective fence. Sadly, four cats were found dead, but I was able to rescue a big white cat covered in blood from the backyard under some rubble, along with another hiding in a bedroom. I scooped them up and brought them to the Town of

Oyster Bay Shelter, where they were treated and adopted. Fittingly, the white one happened to have been named Phoenix.

I didn't see any others that day, so I set up cameras inside what was left of the house. That night I found, to my amazement, that there were several cats wandering around!

But the town scheduled demolition within a few days, even though there was still life inside. The wife tried to stop them but was tied up with her husband, who'd been taken to the hospital with a heart attack. She said on Channel 4 News that she didn't have money to hire a lawyer, and the officials weren't willing to wait.

We mobilized massive protests to delay the razing, but only gained a few days. We had to move fast to get the remaining cats to safety.

During the overnight hours, a few cats, including one we named Star (for being the star of the show), were seen walking in front of my camera, but they all hid from us when we came to the site.

Three of us spent two days searching the house, but there was so much wreckage to move in such little time that I recruited more people.

The day before demo day, we had a large team of around twenty helpers clearing the house, and we found an additional two cats alive, including one named Pepper who was buried under debris and in critical condition. He was rushed to an emergency hospital where he spent two days and, fortunately, survived.

Tragically, despite news media attention from Channel 12, Channel 4, Channel 7, and other outlets, we had not uncovered all the cats by demo day. However, the town agreed to work with us somewhat and took the house down slowly, which allowed volunteers to search the ruins section by section.

All in all, we saved about a dozen cats, including Star, who was found outside after the house had been leveled. Some were transported to Oyster Bay Animal Shelter in Syosset, and others were given to various rescue organizations. The surviving cats who'd been pets had to be put up for adoption, because the family was no longer able to care for them.

The lot remains vacant and people continue to feed the feral cats that live on the property they still call home.

METRO

On November 3, 2023, a Bronx acquaintance heard screams coming from the Metro-North train tracks where a kitten was trapped. There was a twenty-foot wall on each side and no way for it to get out.

She went to Facebook and posted in one of the animal groups, and I was tagged multiple times; she also called and texted me privately.

It was over an hour away, so I was hoping someone closer could help, but because I have experience with tricky rescues like this, they said it was a job for me.

As there seemed to be no other option, I jumped in the car. The contact remained on the scene as I drove and gave me updates to inform me whether the kitten had run away, stayed put, or was rescued before I arrived.

Surprisingly, another friend did show up just as I got there, and we started brainstorming a plan. It was an underground station, with a fair number of commuters, but not rush hour. The kitty was below the platform, on the ground adjacent to the tracks.

Trains were coming within inches of flattening the baby, and the situation was urgent. I wanted to climb down the wall, but quickly realized that probably would have been the last thing I ever did. We needed to find a safe way to do this.

We spoke with the train drivers as they pulled into the stop and flagged down a few conductors to ask if they'd halt the train so we could jump onto the tracks, but sadly, they would not.

We were stumped until we noticed four MTA cops on the opposite platform, and we ran over hoping they'd assist us. And they did!

They contacted their supervisor, who showed up and shut down the power, temporarily paused all trains, and escorted us onto the tracks.

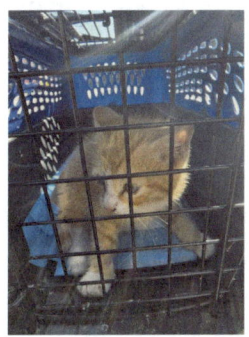

As we approached, I had a net in one hand, and I prayed for the best. Luckily, the kitten did not run, and I quickly scruffed him, then transported him to Last Hope Animal Shelter, where he has since been adopted by the original caller.

He was named Metro.

ETTORE

In the fall of 2021, a man named Salvatore was taking his beloved brown and white cat named Ettore on a flight from JFK Airport. He divides his time between Italy and his Long Island home in Mastic.

Sal checked his cat in as cargo before going through security, and everything seemed to be proceeding normally with no issues, but all of that abruptly changed. After boarding the flight and taking his seat, he was advised by an airport employee that Ettore had escaped from the carrier while being loaded onto the plane and was now lost somewhere on the airport grounds.

When Salvatore landed in Italy the following morning, he made a plea on Facebook for anyone to help locate and secure his cat. A few other people were tagged and responded pretty quickly, but to my knowledge, I was the first animal rescuer on the scene. I hung up fliers and placed cameras in the parking lot area, hoping for a glimpse of the escapee.

After each passing day with no sighting of Ettore, I moved the cameras to different locations within the airport grounds. On the third day, the camera caught someone peeing in the bushes, but there was still no sign of the cat.

We created a group chat with the cat's owner and a few rescue workers, including a noteworthy pet tracker named T. Several volunteers were kind enough to loan additional cameras and manpower, but there was a lot of space to cover.

T and I worked together by focusing on opposite ends of the airport, but there was still no sign of Ettore.

A week later, Salvatore contacted Taylor, the person who ran operations for JFK, and she was able to grant me access to enter restricted areas, including the tarmac.

There were several limitations. I was only allowed to use JFK's traps, and I had to go alone with an escort from airport personnel, so T was not able to help any further. They did let me set up cameras around some restricted areas within the airport, but all we saw was a black cat—not the one we were after.

The following day, a port authority worker noticed a collar at the water's edge alongside the 14,000-foot runway, the longest one at JFK.

We'd already been thinking the cat may have drowned, and it seemed our worst fears might have come true. Despite this, we moved our equipment closer to where Ettore's collar was discovered. About twelve hours later, around 3:00 a.m., we got the surprise of our lives—Ettore walked right in front of the camera, sniffed the food from outside the trap, and then sniffed the camera. But he was still loose.

The following evening, I returned to the airport to freshen the trap with catnip, tuna, sardines, and cat treats to ensure that it would be irresistible.

It worked! My phone started beeping at 4:00 a.m., showing Ettore secured in the cage. I immediately called the airport to make sure there were overnight workers on duty who could escort me out to retrieve Ettore, and there were, so I made the half-hour drive and arrived shortly before 5:00 a.m. After eighteen days, Ettore was safe at last.

The shocking news quickly blew up on Facebook, and his story was picked up by several news media outlets, including NBC, ABC, Fox 5, News 12 Long Island, *Newsday*, and *The New York Post*. Multiple cat rescue websites and smaller media stations also posted it. It went viral!

Ettore was taken to the vet later that day. He had lost three pounds but otherwise only suffered some bruises on his face. The kitty was delivered to Sal's girlfriend's house in Mastic, where he stayed for several months until his owner returned home to see him.

Salvatore continued his biannual travels overseas with his beloved companion, but going forward, Ettore sat up front in the cabin with him on every flight.

Sadly, Ettore passed away three years later from surgical complications while being treated for a urinary blockage. He did not wake up from the anesthesia.

Links to the media coverage of these rescues can be found in the End Notes at the back of this book.

- If at all possible, *never* put a cat—or dog—in a cargo hold. There have been stories of animals dying en route— including when one owner was forced to put her pet in the overhead compartment above her seat. Many airlines will allow one pet per flight to travel in the cabin in a carrier that fits *under* the seat, so make your reservation early. If you cannot bring your furry family member with you on the flight, please leave them with a responsible friend or relative, or arrange for someone to house-sit until you return home.

CHAPTER 7
THE BENEFITS AND OPPORTUNITIES THAT COME WITH BEING ADOPTED BY A CAT

There are two means of refuge from the misery of life—music and cats.
—Albert Einstein

PERKS

BESIDES RIDDING our homes of rodents, there are a multitude of measurable perks we humans receive when we befriend a feline. Children growing up with a family pet learn compassion, responsibility, and empathy, and when life rains its invariably stressful situations on us—at any age—a cat's quiet presence is a comfort. So much entertainment and joy can be found by playing with our furry friends.

Did you know that in some prisons, inmates may adopt a shelter cat? It gives them a humane education by teaching all of the above qualities plus accountability, while providing the cat with a home. Felons with kitty privileges are largely found to become gentler and less aggressive toward other prisoners, and they do not, as some might fear, hurt their companions. These partnerships build self-esteem, and hardened criminals learn to nurture and form strong bonds. Some even make creative toys for their adoptees. The costs of neutering, medical care, and food are paid for by the inmate through their prison work program or family contributions, and the participants show a decrease in recidivism (the chance they will end up back in prison later). It's a healthy avenue to promote kindness and rehabilitation, and the cats win by getting all their needs met and connecting with a loving human benefactor.[18, 19]

It's hip to talk about the cat's meow, but let's delve into the cat's *purr*. We humans reap so many rewards from being purred at. When cats purr, they stimulate a release of oxytocin (sometimes called the "love hormone" because it makes us feel good) and an increased production of endorphins, which are the body's natural opiates. This occurs in both cats and the humans who associate with them.

The frequency of a cat's purr ranges between 25 and 100 Hz and has actually been shown to promote healing. Dr. John Knight reports that his cat parent patients at the Hand and Wrist Institute in Dallas, Texas, experienced improved bone density and strength as well as decreased swelling and a better ability to fight infection.[20]

In addition, the calming vibrations of purring foster relaxation and stress reduction, which decreases the incidence of heart disease. According to Dr. Knight's research, and echoed by the El Gato Veterinary Hospital in Los Gatos, California, cat owners have a 40 percent lower risk of having a heart attack.[21] They also have significantly less hypertension. (Yes, there is a town in Santa Clara County named after cats. *Gatos* means "cats" in Spanish.)

Having a cat can decrease stress and increase your lifespan. An article in the *Journal of Vascular Interventional Neurology* concluded that "a decreased risk for death due to MI [myocardial infarction] and all cardiovascular diseases (including stroke) was observed among persons with cats. Acquisition of cats as domestic pets may represent a novel strategy for reducing the risk of cardiovascular diseases in high-risk individuals."[22]

The American Heart Association also found that cat guardians have a significantly lower incidence of cardiac disease, hypertension, headaches, elevated cholesterol, and anxiety. As you can see, keeping a friendly feline around has many benefits.[23]

All this notwithstanding, folks—please don't stop your cardiac meds and lipid-lowering agents just because you've adopted a cat! Consult your doctor on all things medical.

But, wait—there's more. Cats have been effectively employed in the therapy of autistic children. Introducing a properly selected cat with a calm nature helps socialize children with autism, presumably by alleviating feelings of awkwardness, providing companionship, and boosting confidence.[24, 25]

Pretty cool, right? These whiskered wonders give us so much more than what we originally credited them for when they were using their natural hunting skills to eliminate our need for mousetraps.

> *What greater gift than the love of a cat?*
> —Charles Dickens

All of this presupposes that you have a loving relationship with your cat. But what if you're still getting to know each other or aren't yet sure whether you trust one another? With the exception of pest control, all of these bonuses are based on having a good rapport with your fluffball, and that can take time. Especially if you've adopted a stray or a cat who's been traumatized in the past.

HOW TO MAKE YOUR CAT LIKE YOU

It may seem easier to form a deep friendship with a dog—at least most dog lovers claim this to be so—but bonding with your cat is super special. Particularly because they're pretty choosy about their personal attachments.

Start by respecting who they are and waiting to be invited before you invade their personal space. When you extend just a finger, if your kitty responds by sniffing it and then rubbing her face over the back of your hand (depositing her scent), you can feel confident that it's okay to pet her on her cheeks, but it's important to let her decide when she's ready.

Just as you may not appreciate being smothered by your Great Aunt Bertha's bear hugs *every* time she visits (unless it's a special occasion), your feline compadres do not always welcome being touched whenever it suits your fancy. This only makes every drop of love they lavish on you a blessing, and cats are exceptionally loving companions.

Forming lasting relationships with any living creature, whether human, canine, feline, dolphin, or not a mammal at all, is about spending time together. You're probably not going to be taking walks with your mouser, but *she* likely wants to explore places in your home that you never dreamed could be so interesting. Once you've established basic trust and familiarity, if your cat is fixated on something out the window, put your eyes at her level and look at what she's interested in. When I do this with SammieKat, she becomes deliciously conspiratorial. She'll glance at me and continue to follow the bird / squirrel / leaf with her eyes and even chirp as it moves, head bunting me intermittently to make sure I stay focused as the mental chase progresses.

Each cat's personality is different. Just like one of your children may like basketball, the other might rather stay home and play video games. Get to know what interests your kitty. SammieKat *loves* a project, the more so if I'm sitting on the floor. Whether I'm sorting through greeting cards received from various charities or putting together a piece of furniture, she needs to be in the middle of it.

Last summer, I replaced the kitty condo in "our" bedroom because the sisal was frayed beyond recognition. She lay on the floor next to me and helped me gather the different screws and then sat inside the hidey-holes while I was trying to construct them around her. Naturally, once it was complete and all set up, it held very little interest for her, but there was definitely a lot of bonding that went into the assembly.

And don't forget to play with them! Birds filled with catnip on a wand, balls that rattle, and pillow toys they can grab with their front paws and tear to pieces with their hind legs will give them entertainment and confidence in themselves as the best hunter in the territory. Sharing these fun times makes you even more special to them. Please see the section in Chapter 5 about play, which is heavily infused with Dr. Geller's input.

COMMUNICATING WITH YOUR CAT

Do you talk to your cats? Okay, sure you do, but do you expect them to understand?

I used to be convinced that Zilly was a C student. He just didn't seem to get what I wanted from him for the longest time. The fact that he was a chowhound, topping out at eighteen and a half pounds when he was diagnosed with diabetes, is pertinent here, but "smart" didn't seem to be part of his personality profile.

One day after our dog died, Zilly was begging at the kitchen table. It was something the canine never allowed him to do—too much competition, I guess—so this was Zilly's moment. He was being very persistent.

Curious, I turned my chair toward him and held a piece of chicken between my fingers. "Sit," I said.

He gave me a bewildered, I-don't-know-what-you're-talking-about look and pointed his nose at the morsel in my hand. We stayed deadlocked like that for several seconds.

I cocked my head to the side and said again, "Sit."

"Who, me?" he seemed to say, but as the seconds ticked by, his expression changed to a glare. Too bad I didn't get it on camera, because it clearly said, "You've got to be kidding." He circled my legs a few times and came back to gaze earnestly at the food.

"Zilly," I said, "you lived with that dog for eleven years. I know you know what 'sit' means."

The next thirty seconds were a staring match. His eyes went from the "Who, me?" look, to "She knows... she knows I know..." Then, to undeniable annoyance.

Finally, Zilly, the *un*exceptional pupil, sat down. Wow. I gave him the chicken, and he popped back up immediately to circle my chair.

Of course, he wanted more.

I repeated this two more times, and each time he sat more quickly—and got up again more quickly, as if hoping no one had seen, and definitely looked put out. I called my son downstairs to demonstrate.

"Mom! You made him break the cat code! Don't do that to him."

I couldn't stop laughing. *Cat code*. Of course, because no one expects a cat to obey a command.

But afterward, even though I never asked it of him again, we all knew the truth: Zilly was perhaps the smartest of all. Only, it had not *served* him to let us perceive that.

I'm not sure that made Zilly like me, but it did bring us closer by making other communication possible. I expected him to understand more, and he stopped pretending he didn't.

Midnight's linguistic talents are remarkable, and not just because she has always vocalized to me. When she had surgery to remove her bladder stones, she'd only been indoors for a few months. Getting her into a carrier then was not difficult because she was in so much pain, but getting her back to the vet for suture removal was a whole different story.

By cutting off other accesses, I managed to herd her into the bathroom where her litter box was, and closed the door. Placing her open kennel on the floor, I sat down on top of the commode, and... we talked. Literally.

She stood on her hind legs from inside the tub with her paws on the rim and meowed apprehensively, and I explained to her as best I could that we had to get her stitches out. I pointed to her and pointed to my belly and then pointed back at her. I made no move to pick her up—she'd been very clear that she found such behavior nothing short of offensive, so I waited. She continued to meow and I continued to present my case.

Unbelievably, after three or four minutes of this, she jumped over the ledge and voluntarily walked into the carrier.

As soon as I closed the gate, however, the meowing grew louder and more persistent—it became a yowl. I imagined she was thinking, "I'll never do *that* again!"

Here's another example of cats recognizing exactly what we're saying.

SammieKat was beyond miserable over my having adopted Midnight, and I almost rehomed the stray Tuxedo to appease my senior cat. But after the x-ray revealed the two pellets she'd somehow survived, I couldn't bring myself to shuffle her around anymore. What if her new owner gave her away or turned her out *again*?

I sighed and looked at my sad little Samster. "I'm sorry, you're going to have to get over it," I said. "She's staying."

Then I sat down next to her and agreed that she was 100 percent correct, we do not need another cat. But this cat needs us, and we have to help her.

Surprisingly, Sam got the message. I know she did, although she wasn't happy about it. The growling stopped, and she began to direct her anger at me instead.

One day, she appeared to be contemplating mischief while staring into Midnight's room, and I simply said, "Sam."

She turned to walk instead toward the stairs but pivoted midway, looked me straight in the eyes, and hissed *at me* before continuing down the hall.

Another time, they were observing each other from across the hallway, or what I call the Demilitarized Zone. Midnight was hunkered down and alert, ears flat, and tail wrapped tightly around her body, while SammieKat's dander was up, her back was slightly arched even lying down, and her tail was swishing rapidly. Although there'd never been any physical contact between them, it looked like an altercation could be in the works.

"Guys!" I said, loud enough to startle them. "You're sisters! Can't you be friends—or at least leave each other alone?"

Both postures changed immediately. Midnight sat up tall and pretty with her chin tucked all the way, as if to say, "Sure, I can do that." SammieKat's fur dropped, her spine lowered, and her tail quieted as she settled into a loaf position. But her face scowled and looked for all the world like she was muttering, "I don't want to."

I believe our cats grasp our intent even if they can't translate our words. Of course, being able to read their body language helps us predict what activity is imminent. But when our little felines realize we understand them, they're more likely to participate in the conversation.

The resolution in my household is still voluntary self-separation. I don't put a gate up anymore unless I'm going to be away overnight, and I've found that as long as I spend more alone time cuddling and playing with SammieKat than I do with Midnight, my senior puddy is mollified. (I think she times me.)

EXPLORING ALL OPTIONS

I wish I had known Dr. Geller when I adopted Midnight, but I did not. I had already queried a different behaviorist, an emotion code therapist, and tried pheromone sprays and collars, but nothing worked. Finally, I enlisted help from an animal communicator. I don't understand how they function, especially since it was all done over the telephone, but I was desperate. Ironically, she was possibly the most helpful of all.

I was worried that Sammie might be feeling threatened or jealous, but the communicator said no. SammieKat sees herself as my equal, as if we are sisters. In her eyes, the house belongs to both of us, and she looks down on Midnight as some "alley cat" I dragged in without her consent. My consultant also recommended I try Bach's Flower Essences.

The whole thing was entertaining, if not enlightening, although I can well imagine Sammie feeling both of those things. I was, however, more than slightly mortified by the insinuated condescension. I thought prejudices were learned, not inherited. I even proceeded to scold Sammie: "We do *not* judge people by where they come from or the color of their fur!"

My Persian Tortie was unmoved, but the Bach's did help a lot. As of now, the two cats stay in their respective territories except for those sporadic moments when Sam strolls onto Midnight's turf and struts around as if to remind her, "This is really *my* room. I'm just *letting* you stay here."

A word about flower essences like Bach's. I can't speak to any scientific evidence, as these are homeopathic formulations, but I used one of their distillates for my Golden Retriever decades ago. He was terrified of thunder, and a one-hundred-pound dog in a state of panic every time a storm hits is no joke. He'd squeeze himself into places that were not big enough to accommodate him, resulting in cracked cabinets and beds "walking" across the room. After three weeks of regular Bach's Remedies, his fear evaporated. Or, at least, his behavior normalized. The effects lasted for years.

Getting Bach's into a cat is a bit trickier. SammieKat won't touch canned or table food; she *only* eats dry kibble (or rubber bands, hair ties, plastic, tissues... you get the idea; fortunately, there's an endoscopy center for cats on Long Island). She does drink water, but not the whole bowl, and I didn't want to irritate her by dripping medicine in her mouth three to four times a day. However, it is acceptable to rub a little of the essence on the inner membrane of the ear, and that has worked wonders. Just be very careful not to let any of it trickle down *inside* your cat's ear.

From what I've read, Jackson Galaxy's Spirit Essences are similarly based on alternative medicine, and his ads state that he has tailored his tinctures specifically to cats. I have not used any, so I can't endorse them. I'm just mentioning it for your information.

- Befriending a cat is good for your mental and physical health.

CHAPTER 8
IT TAKES A VILLAGE

NO ONE PERSON can care for all our community cats by themselves. But you can help.

People like Dr. Marge Goldin, Dr. Rachel Geller, and John DeBacker are godsends to us and cats everywhere, indoors and out, as are the many shelters and vets who give deep discounts when treating homeless moggies. But there are just too many little critters in need out there for a few individuals to handle, and the cost of caring for them all is astronomical. Sure, felines made it on their own out in the wilderness, but civilization, by its very nature, limits their food availability by driving out their prey, and both our urban and suburban environments come with many dangers. Landscapers, cars, and the pesticides we use threaten cats' lives every day. Not to mention cruel human beings.

Hopefully, if you're reading this, you're thinking about how you can support their cause. Donations are extremely important, and you've already made a small cash bequest just by purchasing this book, since a percentage of the royalties goes through John DeBacker to distribute to his affiliate, LICKS. These contributions to the Long Island CAT & KITTEN Solution, a 501c3 nonprofit organization, help offset the cost of rescue operations and veterinary bills for injured animals.

Money is needed in many other nonprofits, like Tender Loving Cats (tenderlovingcats.org). TLC is an all-volunteer organization that performs TNR on neighborhood cats through their Prevent a Litter program. Funds are desperately needed for the veterinary bills associated with surgery and vaccination of each community cat that goes through their system.

All no-kill shelters need to house and feed cats as they wait for adoption. This costs money and more; it also requires *space*, which is an understated commodity. And consider that the larger the building, the higher the operating expenses, and the greater the need for your financial assistance.

Tender Loving Cats functions as a foster-based adoption agency. They have no physical site requiring a mortgage and electricity, but this means they can only take kittens and cats who have a foster willing to care for them while awaiting their forever home. Once admitted into the adoption program, these little furballs are, of course, spayed/neutered and vaccinated, but also dewormed and microchipped, and their professional headshots are placed on the website. Although adoption fees offset some of these bills, if the cat gets sick while in the program and requires extra medical care, TLC covers them, which could amount to thousands of dollars.

Sadly, many cats across the country are returned after adoption because the new pet parents are frustrated by natural feline behavior or cannot afford items needed to catify their home to make it cat-friendly, like toys or kitty condos. Simple measures, as we read about earlier, can transform a nightmare into a rewarding, fulfilling relationship between cats and their humans.

Dr. Geller's foundation, All Cats All the Time (drrachelcatbehavior.com), provides free cat behavior counseling in her mission to keep cats and people together; an alternative to those who would otherwise turn their furry family out onto the street for scratching the sofa. She does not charge for her services and thus relies heavily on the generosity of her clients. She uses their gifts to provide catifying home equipment to those who cannot afford it, and it can mean the difference between a cat having a loving home or being abandoned. I hope you will support her.

Money donated to 501c3 nonprofits, like Dr. Geller's and Tender Loving Cats, is tax deductible.

By taking the time to learn about outdoor cats, their needs, and how to care for them yourself, you can take a huge burden off the shoulders of these operations that cannot be everywhere at once.

For example, say you've been feeding a cat in your backyard for months, and you realize that he should be neutered and vaccinated, even though you may not be able to take him in. Or maybe he looks injured and you want to get him to a vet. Rather than asking someone else to snare him, hopefully, after reading the chapter on trapping, you'll be more comfortable catching him yourself. If you borrow a trap from a shelter, you can take your little visitor on your own (or with a cat-loving friend) to one of the numerous vets who offer reduced fees for treating community cats. Then release him back to his usual feeding ground.

To find resources in your neighborhood, try joining a local Facebook group that caters to cats and ask. They will likely be able to point you in the right direction. Google will undoubtedly have multiple suggestions that you can evaluate by asking in the community.

Adoption is the ultimate act of compassion, and as we saw, it feeds your own soul as well as saves a cat. In my tradition, we say, "When you save one life, it is as if you saved an entire world."

Even if you cannot make the long-term commitment to adopt, can you foster a cat and help acclimate them to human affection? If you have an area in your house or basement that could be turned into a safe room for a few weeks, you can rehabilitate a homeless kitty. When shelters are full, if a cat can stay with you while a good match is found, it would take a load off the shoulders of the rescue organizations, and you'd get to spend some time with a little Leo in need without making a lifelong commitment.

Many of the kittens that are taken in aren't ready to meet their forever family. Either they're too young or just need time to become accustomed to humans before they can be put up for adoption. Fostering isn't just about providing a temporary residence; it involves holding and petting, and letting these little tikes experience the natural sounds and energy of life indoors.

Fostering cats at home

What about becoming a volunteer? Shelters need loving humans to feed and play with their resident kitties, make follow-up phone calls to recent adopters, transport sick cats to the vet, help orchestrate fundraisers, and perform a myriad of administrative tasks that keep the organization running. If you don't have money to spare, there's so much you can still do in your free time.

Or—you might have a job opening for a cat! TLC is one of several associations that offer a barn cat adoption program. When a feral cat is removed from a dangerous situation but cannot be socialized, they could be relocated to a barn, a ranch, or a warehouse if one is available. There, the cat can earn his kibble by performing rodent control measures without the need for pesticides or traps. This aligns perfectly with the original motivations for the cat-human liaison and could be a boon for your business. The animals receive care and shelter in a safe environment, and you, the business owner, get your needs met for the price of a few cases of canned cat food and a litter box. And that feral just might come around one day and decide he wants to be friends. You never know.

In addition, just educating yourself about feline behavior and cat language is a big help. Thank you for reading this far and doing so! Explaining to your neighbors why they should never approach a strange animal quickly or raise their hand above its head to pet them can avert injuries and prevent bad feelings, thereby keeping your colony welcome in the community. Knowing how to introduce a new cat into your home, whether as a solo pet or to join your other four-legged companions, saves aggravation and may prevent you from returning the cat. You may even find yourself coaching a new cat parent.

Whether you can embrace a new family member, perform the trapping, pay the vet bill, foster a cat prior to adoption, or make a donation, you are helping the entire community of cats and cat-loving humans.

Since you've bought this book, I want to acknowledge you for your compassion and desire to help in whatever way you can. Your love heals.

CHAPTER 9
FUN FACTS ABOUT CATS

I CAN'T SIGN off without sharing a few fun facts ideal for cool cocktail conversations. Here are some things every cat lover should know.

Deafness linked to coloring: It is suspected that up to 80 percent of white cats with blue eyes are deaf.[27]

Definitions: A group of cats is called a clowder. An intact male cat is called a tom, and a fertile female is called a molly or a queen. A cat-loving human is called an ailurophile.

Ears: The feline auditory system is a biological marvel. Each cat ear has 32 muscles and can pivot independently 180 degrees. They hear much higher frequencies and from farther away than either dogs or humans. At a distance of 3 feet, cats are able to distinguish between sounds 3 inches apart in 0.06 seconds.[26, 27] There's also an accessory pouch at the base of a cat's ear called Henry's Pouch, but there's no consensus on exactly what function it serves.

Eyesight: Cats are notoriously farsighted, meaning they don't see well up close. They rely largely on their sense of smell and their whiskers to find what is a few inches in front of them.

Gender: Calico cats are always female. This is because the trait for tricolor markings is X-linked and recessive, so it needs two X chromosomes to be expressed. The only exception is a mutation called Klinefelter's syndrome, in which there are three chromosomes present, written as XXY. This occurs in one in five thousand cats, and those are predominantly sterile.

Hunting: All cats are master predators and rely heavily on stealth. When they stalk their prey, they walk so that their hind paws land in the footprints of their front feet, making their tracks harder to recognize.

Jumping: Cats can jump six to eight feet in the air, or about six times their height. (I experienced this the first time I tried to get Midnight into a carrier.)

Nose prints: Cats' nose prints are as specific as our fingerprints.

Pheromones: The information left by rubbing their scent glands on trees and furniture not only tells another cat whether they are male or female, in heat or not, but also identifies them almost as individually as a DNA pattern.

Physiology: Cats can drink seawater! Hopefully you know that humans will dehydrate from salt water, so if you're stranded in a boat on the ocean, drinking the water around you will only kill you faster. But cats' kidneys can filter out the salt—assuming they do not have any renal disease.

NOTE: that's not to say that you should—or would—ever give them salt water, nor polluted or algae-ridden water, which could be toxic. In fact, most cats have an instinct to avoid stagnant puddles. Once indoors, especially if trained from an early age, they usually consent to drink from the bowl you put out for them, although SammieKat much prefers to sit on the bathroom counter and slake her thirst from the running faucet.

Running: Domestic cats can run 30 to 40 mph. No wonder you can't catch them.

Sleeping: Domestic cats sleep for an average of thirteen to fourteen hours a day.

Spirituality: Cats have long been hailed as spirit creatures, connected to supernatural forces and shrouded in mysticism, deification, or witchcraft, with the ability to both ward off and welcome evil. No doubt due to their independent, mysterious, and sometimes haughty personalities, coupled with an endless curiosity.

Tears: A cat's tears contain a pigment called porphyrin that turns them reddish-brown, or rust-colored. The first time I saw this, I called my vet in a panic—I thought my cat's eye was bleeding.

Toes: Some cats have a sixth toe on one or more paws from a mutation called polydactyly. Ernest Hemingway was known for loving these unusual animals, which were believed to be magical and bring good fortune, perhaps due to their superior ability to climb and catch rodents. If you tour the Hemingway Home and Museum in Key West, Florida, you can visit with roughly fifty cats, about half of whom have this anomaly. All are descendants of his original polydactyl named Snow White.

Whiskers: A cat's whiskers are as sensitive as our human fingertips. They act like radar to detect and interpret motion, and help felines navigate their surroundings. By measuring wind currents, whether caused by a fleeing rodent or created by their own movement as air bounces off an object, whiskers locate and identify the elements in their environment.

Muzzle whiskers also guide them by calculating the width of openings the mouser may want to crawl into. This sensitivity is why well-designed cat bowls are shallow; it's to avoid overstimulating the whiskers if they rub against the sides. Cats even have whiskers on their tails and in their ears.[28]

And last but not least...

Aerodynamics: We've all heard that cats always land on their feet. Well, not always, and do *not* go throwing your cat out of a window. I mean, unless the house is on fire and you're jumping right behind him. But here's the science: The spine of a feline is super flexible, and during a fall, the righting reflex is activated. First, they twist one way to tuck their front paws and increase their angular momentum—much like a figure skater does—then they corkscrew around in the other direction and spread their rear legs to increase their inertia (reduce their spin). Once their head is in the correct position relative to the Earth, they repeat the process with the hind legs until they are fully righted.

All objects that fall to the ground from great heights eventually reach a maximum speed when the air resistance cancels out the acceleration of gravity. This happens earlier for a cat than for a human because they weigh so much less. Once cats reach that terminal velocity and no longer feel the force of acceleration, they tend to relax and extend their legs outward to increase their surface area—kind of like opening a parachute. Still, they can reach a speed of 60 to 70 mph![29]

My scientific brain finds this fascinating, but, again—*please—don't throw your cats out of windows or off the roof!*

Thank you for reading this book and for caring about cats. When these singularly refined creatures grace us with their love, they can open our hearts and heal our souls. Your contribution to their well-being will be repaid a hundred times over.

If you found this book valuable, would you please write a review? It helps others decide whether this guide would be helpful to them and may encourage them to support our feline friends, indoors and out.

Here's a final fun fact, this one for humans: People who read *fiction* have been found to have less chance of developing dementia. Maybe because it engages both aspects of the brain, analytical and emotional, and our minds automatically follow plots, subplots, characters, and motivations simultaneously. Who doesn't like a good story?

I am primarily a fiction author, and I invite you to pick up a copy of *The Meraki Effect,* a sci-fi suspense novel that features a Maine Coon as a primary supporting character. He doesn't speak (of course not, he's a cat), but he may be the only one who can save the colony of Earth refugees from annihilation. The story is complete in itself, but if you like book sets, the saga continues in *The Meraki NeXus.*

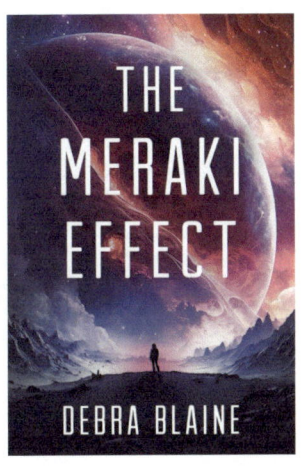

ACKNOWLEDGMENTS

There are so many people I want to thank for contributing to this book, it's hard to know where to start. Please know that the sequence of mentions does not reflect any particular order.

Dr. Mitchell Kornet, DVM

Thank you first of all for the great care you have given to my four-legged family over the last two decades, and the time you always take to explain their maladies in medical diagnostic terms that I can apply in making well-informed decisions.

And thank you especially for reading this book—and all my books! While there is no medical advice within these pages, giving your veterinarian's stamp of approval assured me I wasn't leading anyone astray (pun intended) regarding basic concepts and preventive measures. The frosting on the cake is your phenomenal written endorsement, which I have proudly placed inside and on the back cover, as well as on the detail page for *Whiskers*.

Dr. Marge Goldin, DSW

First and foremost, thank you for your friendship over the years, which has grown since starting this project. You made it possible for Midnight to come in out of the wild and find a loving home, and my little Tuxedo and I will be forever grateful. But there's more.

You provided extensive tutelage on trapping, which enabled me to write a hopefully useful primer for beginners, and you've been here to bounce ideas off of. Let's not forget the couple of photoshoots with uncooperative cats, one amid SammieKat's growling and hissing, as she expressed her distaste for having her nap interrupted. It was a perfect example of how vital it is to know when your cat is serious about being aggressive or just complaining loudly.

John DeBacker

Thank you for everything you do for cats and other vulnerable animals. You have saved countless lives. Although, if you were my son, my heart would be in my mouth with each perilous rescue you venture upon. It has been a pleasure and a privilege to work with you on this book, and my hope is that it will assist and inspire our many fellow cat lovers to care for the community cats on Long Island and around the world.

Dr. Rachel Geller, EdD

Your generosity is beyond compare. The service you provide for cat parents, free of charge, is responsible for keeping cats homed and humans happy. I'm so glad I took a chance and sent you that email asking if you might write the foreword and contribute to this book. Your input has been invaluable, plus I now have a new friend. I hope one day we'll be in the same city and can meet for lunch.

Debbie Kurzban, JD

I'm immensely grateful for our forty years of friendship, including your eagerness to be a beta reader for my books. Thank you for your keen, constructive edits. This wasn't my usual fiction, but as a volunteer for wildlife preservation and a dog fosterer, I'd hoped you'd be willing to take on another manuscript. You never let me down.

Ellen Gelerman

As always, you always come through for me; this time it was for my last-minute panic over choosing photos for *Whiskers*. We raised our kids together, and now write our books together while still sharing the trials and tribulations of life these past thirty-plus years—even across several states.

SammieKat

You've been my BFFF for the last fifteen years. I am so blessed to have your love—especially when you let me rest my head on your soft, fluffy fur while you deliver purrfect endorphin infusions directly into my brain. We've been through so much together, and I'm counting on you sticking around for many more years to come.

Midnight!

My dear little Midnight, you are the original scaredy cat, and with good reason. How can I thank you for choosing me, adopting me, and teaching me that faith can overcome fear? In four years, not once have you swatted or bitten me, and I can count your hisses on one hand. Despite all the trauma and suffering you've been through, somehow your soul has remained steadfastly gentle and pure. This book is possible because of you, but more importantly, my whole life is brighter because of you.

Zilly

Gone but never forgotten, you are memorialized here in these pages. Browsing through old photos reminded me of your cuddliness, silliness, and adorable wise-guy looks. I miss you, buddy.

Rocco

Dear little Rocco, a resident feral of our community. I'm so glad you found a comforting place that suits you, where you are now well-fed and have a house all your own. Thanks for posing for a photoshoot. Since you've been known to meow now and then, I predict you will one day be an indoor house pet in your benefactor's home.

North Shore Animal League America

I cannot close without expressing my gratitude to the North

Shore Animal League, which took in SammieKat as a teeny tiny tot from an overcrowded shelter in Albany in 2009 and enabled us to become a family. NSAL does an amazing service, not just locally here on Long Island, but by accepting homeless cats and dogs from all over the country, particularly when a catastrophe has struck. Some humanitarians may feel this organization is so big, it does not need donations, but it's *because* of their size and scope that its need for charitable gifts is even greater. I hope you'll put them on your list and give generously.

Vets, town shelters, and good Samaritans

Gratitude is especially due to the multitude of shelters, veterinarians, and good Samaritans who serve the welfare of cats and deeply discount their prices.

In my tradition, we do not consider that we humans are meant to dominate the Earth. We believe we are here as caretakers, or executors, if you will. We have been charged with caring for life on this planet, and, in my opinion, have drifted far off track. However, I take heart in the many heroes who rise to the task by nurturing, saving, and loving our animals, especially our cats. Clearly, that includes many of you.

ABOUT THE AUTHOR

Debra Baine, MD, CPC, CMT, is a physician, three-time award-winning author, certified life coach, and certified master trainer.

Mostly, she writes thrillers, dystopian suspense, and science fiction, which invariably include animals—usually cats—in their cast of characters. However, in the past year, she has published several reference resources, such as this title.

In *The Meraki Effect*, the first of the *Meraki Files* duology, the fate of an entire space colony rests on a Maine Coon's love for a ten-year-old girl. It's available on Amazon and Barnes & Noble.

Since 2019, Debra has served as a stress management life coach, helping clients disengage from the degrading pressures of society, whose values seem to be spiraling into materialism and hostility. Through rediscovering their hearts' purpose, they thrive.

In addition, she mentors writers at all stages, from crafting their first draft to tightening their prose, and guides them through the self-publishing process. She's helped dozens of authors professionally publish their books on their own timelines with minimal expense.

Feel free to reach out to her for information at DebraBlaine@DebraBlaine.com if you're interested in any of these services, or check out her website: AllThingsWriting.com.

Dr. Blaine practiced family and urgent care medicine for thirty-three years until the dysfunctional state of our healthcare system became unbearable for her. In January of 2023, she pivoted to work full-time as a writer and a coach, where she feels she can make more of a difference in people's lives.

As a lifelong animal lover and cat parent since the age of ten, she's often been heard saying that she should have been a vet. But what most people don't know is that upon graduating high school, she *really* wanted to be a forest ranger. Her parents strongly objected, so she went on to study liberal arts and ultimately, medicine. She has now come full circle. Back to nature, back to animals, and back to the arts as an author.

Debra is a proud grandma and lives on Long Island with her two rescue cats, SammieKat and Midnight—who unfortunately, will not sit together for a dual photo op.

DR. RACHEL GELLER

Rachel Geller, Ed.D., is the Founder and President of *All Cats All the Time*, a 501c3 nonprofit dedicated to preventing the surrender and abandonment of cats. She offers cat behavior counseling free of charge to shelters and cat owners who cannot otherwise afford it. You can find her online at drrachelcatbehavior.com.

Rachel is certified as a: Cat Behavior and Retention Specialist, Surrender Prevention Specialist, Humane Education Specialist, Pet Chaplain®, Fear Free Shelter Specialist, American Association of Feline Practitioners Cat Friendly Veterinary Advocate, DEI in Animal Welfare Advancement, and RedRover Empathy Reader. She is currently a cat behaviorist for shelters all over the world, working with adopters, training shelter volunteers, and instituting surrender prevention programs. She also provides individual cat behavior help to cat parents. She has presented to numerous animal welfare groups.

Rachel is the creator of the Surrender Prevention Specialist certification course, which is approved by the National Animal Control Association for CE credits and Maddie's Fund for scholarships.

Rachel is also the author of the webinar "Activities for Inclusion" for the Association of Professional Humane Educators. This webinar presents instructions and techniques that animal shelters can follow to include volunteers from the special needs population. She was a contributing author to "The Ark Project – Jewish Initiative for Animals," which focuses on the humane treatment of animals.

Rachel is a panelist for the Chaplaincy Innovation Lab through Brandeis University as a Pet Chaplain.

Her book, *Saving the World, One Cat at a Time*, was written to help resolve cats' behavioral and emotional problems and create harmonious relationships between cats and their owners.

JOHN DEBACKER

John DeBacker is a famed cat crusader, known for daring rescues under near-impossible circumstances. He is currently Coprincipal Officer of LICKS, Long Island Cat & Kitten Solution, which is a 501c3 nonprofit organization in Bellmore, NY. He's certified in TNR, was trained in Pet CPR, and was awarded a Certificate of Appreciation from the Suffolk County SPCA.

John grew up in Seaford, NY, and has always loved animals. Although his parents kept dogs as pets, he always wanted a cat, so directly out of high school, he began volunteering for Bobbi and the

Strays in Freeport by socializing homeless cats. While he was working there, a neighbor died, and their daughter turned the four house cats out on the street. John helped trap and get them to safety, an act that became a pivotal moment in his life.

Since then, it's been his mission to help community cats who are in danger, in need of a home, or require medical care. He has made a name for himself beyond Long Island to the entire Tri-State area, across the country, and has even been featured internationally in Peru and Brazil.

John is most active on Facebook with thousands of cat-loving followers and has been interviewed by a multitude of national news stations. Articles have been written about him in the New York Post and Newsday.

He lives on Long Island with three cats of his own: rescues, of course.

Connect with him on Facebook:
https://www.facebook.com/john.debacker.50

DR. MARGE GOLDIN

Marge Goldin, DSW, currently serves on the Board of Directors of Tender Loving Cats (TLC) and is the Coordinator of the Prevent A Litter Program. She developed the Recycling 4 Rescue initiative, which raises money by redeeming beverage containers with a New York State deposit. This program is unique because it utilizes volunteer adults with disabilities, thereby giving them meaningful work to do. More information on these and other projects can be found on the TLC website:
   TenderLoving Cats.org

Marge has been an animal lover all her life, since getting permission to adopt her first cat at the age of five. After retiring from Sachem Schools as a school social worker, she began following cat rescue Facebook pages, which led to her first foster litter for Tender Loving Cats, and then becoming a colony caretaker. At that colony, where some of the cats were not spayed or neutered, she learned how to trap. Since that time, her involvement with TLC has steadily increased.

Marge lives on Long Island with her husband, her three cats, and her cat colony.

ALSO BY DEBRA BLAINE

1. CODE BLUE: *The Other End of the Stethoscope*
2. *Undue Influences*
3. *Beyond the Pillars of Salt*
4. *The Meraki Effect* (Book 1 of *The Meraki Files*)
5. *The Meraki Nexus* (Book 2 of *The Meraki Files*)
6. *Deadly Algorithm* (Available only through her newsletter, *Ink & Scalpel*)
7. *Animal Mandala Patterns: Stress Relief Coloring Book For Adults and Teens*
8. *The WriteR Stuff: Step-by-Step Guide to Self-publishing and Worldwide Distribution*
9. *The WriteR Stuff: Secret Sauce of Writing Fiction*

END NOTES

CITATIONS

1. Chantelle Fowler, "8 Ways People Are Like Cats: Genetics, Traits & More," Catster, March 6, 2025, www.catster.com/lifestyle/how-are-people-like-cats.

2. Alley Cat Allies, "History of the Domestic Cat," accessed April 24, 2025, www.allcycat.org/resources/the-natural-history-of-the-cat.

3. Rosicrucian Egyptian Museum, "Deities in Ancient Egypt—Bastet," accessed April 24, 2025, https://egyptianmuseum.org/deities-Bastet.

4. Viovet of UK, "Russian Blue Cats," accessed April 24, 2025, www.viovet.co.uk/breed_information/1-66/Russian-Blue.

5. Casey Smith, "Cats Domesticated Themselves, Ancient DNA Shows," *National Geographic*, June 19, 2017, www.nationalgeographic.com/science/article/domesticated-cats-dna-genetics-pets-science.

6. Gary M. Landsberg, "Normal Social Behavior in Cats," Merck Veterinary Manual, modified September 2024, www.merckvetmanual.com/cat-owners/behavior-of-cats/normal-social-behavior-in-cats.

7. The Royal (Dick) School of Veterinary Studies, "Understanding Feline Social Structure," University of Edinburgh, 2019 (v1.2), https://edwebcontent.ed.ac.uk/sites/default/files/atoms/files/1._understanding_feline_social_structure.pdf.

8. Feral Cat Spay/Neuter Project, "Myths & Controversies," accessed April 24, 2025, www.feralcatproject.org/myths-controversies.

9. Feral Cat Focus of WNY, "Colony Management—FIV and FeLV," accessed April 24, 2025, https://feralcatfocus.org/colony-management-fiv-felv.

10. Alley Cat Allies, "Rabies: A Public Health Victory," accessed April 24, 2025, www.alleycat.org/resources/rabies-a-public-health-victory.

11. Dennis C. Turner, "The Mechanics of Social Interactions Between Cats and Their Owners," *Frontiers in Veterinary Science* 8 (2021): 650143, https://pmc.ncbi.nlm.nih.gov/articles/PMC8044293.

12. Brenda Griffin, "Returning Healthy Feral Cats," Humane Pro, *Animal Sheltering* Magazine, January/February 2013, https://humanepro.org/magazine/articles/returning-healthy-feral-cats.

13. Jackson Galaxy, "Quivering, Wagging, Puffed Up: What Is Your Cat's Tail Trying to Tell You?" posted September 9, 2023, YouTube, www.youtube.com/watch?v=JLi3Z_Mlshk.

14. John Knight, "Is a Cat's Purr Actually Helpful to Our Bones?," The Hand and Wrist Institute, accessed April 24, 2025, https://handandwristinstitute.com/is-a-cats-purr-actually-helpful-to-our-bones.

15. Beth Dokolasa, "Decoding Cat Body Language," Cat Care Society, April 23, 2023, www.catcaresociety.org/decoding-cat-body-language.

16. HHSA Tulare County Animal Services, "Don't Kit-Nap Kittens," accessed May 16, 2025, https://tcanimalservices.org/animalservices/resources/dont-kit-nap-kittens/.

17. PAWS, "Introducing Your Cat to a New Cat," ASPCA,

accessed April 24, 2025, www.paws.org/resources/introducing-cat-to-cat.

18. Alley Cat Allies, "Trap-Neuter-Return (TNR): Prison Cats," accessed April, 24, 2025, www.alleycat.org/our-work/trap-neuter-return/prison-cats.

19. Christopher Zoukis, "Indiana State Prison Cat Therapy Program," Elizabeth Franklin-Best P.C., January 4, 2012, https://federalcriminaldefenseattorney.com/indiana-state-prison-cat-therapy-program-html.

20. John Knight, "Is a Cat's Purr Actually Helpful to Our Bones?," The Hand and Wrist Institute, accessed April 24, 2025, https://handandwristinstitute.com/is-a-cats-purr-actually-helpful-to-our-bones.

21. El Gato Veterinary Hospital, "The Fascinating Science Behind a Cat's Purr," July 31, 2023, https://elgatovet.com/blog/the-fascinating-science-behind-a-cats-purr.

22. Adnan I. Qureshi et al., "Cat Ownership and the Risk of Fatal Cardiovascular Diseases: Results from the Second National Health and Nutrition Examination Study Mortality Follow-Up Study," *Journal of Vascular and Interventional Neurology* 2, no. 1 (2009): 132–35, https://pmc.ncbi.nlm.nih.gov/articles/PMC3317329.

23. Glenn N. Levine et al., "Pet Ownership and Cardiovascular Risk: A Scientific Statement from the American Heart Association," *Circulation* 127, no. 23 (2013), https://doi.org/10.1161/CIR.0b013e31829201e1.

24. Betti Wilson, "Cats and Autism: Improving Social Skills in Children," *Autism Parenting* Magazine, February 17, 2025, www.autismparentingmagazine.com/cats-help-children-with-autism.

25. Gretchen K. Carlisle et al., "Exploratory Study of Cat Adoption in Families of Children with Autism: Impact on Children's Social Skills and Anxiety," *Journal of Pediatric Nursing* 58 (2021): 28–35, https://doi.org/10.1016/j.pedn.2020.11.011.

26. LizaKittyBootCamp, "How Well Cats Hear: A Quick

Guide," *Tails and Tips*, November 15, 2023, https://lizskittyboot camp.com/2023/11/15/how-well-cats-hear.

27. Jamie Lovejoy, "Listen Up to These Fascinating Facts About Your Cat's Ears," PetMD, February 8, 2023, www.petmd.com/cat/general-health/cat-ear-facts.

28. Anne Dagner et al., "Why Do Cats Have Whiskers?," VCA Animal Hospitals, accessed April 24, 2025, https://vcahospitals.com/know-your-pet/why-do-cats-have-whiskers.

29. Manon Bischoff, "Why Do Cats Land on Their Feet? Physics Explains," *Scientific American*, July 24, 2023, www.scientificamerican.com/article/why-do-cats-land-on-their-feet-physics-explains.

JOHN DEBACKER'S RESCUE STORIES IN THE NEWS

Oakley: *USA Today, Animalkind*; November 12, 2024; "Watch a rescuer's cat-like reflexes pluck a kitten from mid-air after a scary fall."https://www.usatoday.com/videos/life/animalkind/2024/11/12/tree-climbing-heros-quick-reflexes-save-kitten-from-terrifying-tumble/76227085007/

Merry: *EYEWITNESS NEWS*; Pets & Animals; "NJ man rescues cat with head stuck in jar on Christmas," December 27, 2023 https://abc7ny.com/animal-rescue-cat-in-jar-cats-head-stuck-christmas-miracle/14228930/

Wanda: *Inside Edition's YouTube Channel*; "Hero Saves Kitten Running on Busy Long Island Parkway" https://youtu.be/z4BAZ2ZxtRo?si=X0Bc25GvXCMx-kDj

Ettore: *NY Post*, September 21, 2021 "Long Island cat spends 3 weeks on JFK runways after escaping flight," https://nypost.com/2021/09/21/long-island-cat-spent-3-weeks-on-jfk-runways-after-escaping/

Metro: *BronxTimes*, "Near cat-astrophe: Kitten halts Bronx train Thursday morning," November 3, 2022, https://www.bxtimes.com/near-cat-astrophe-kitten-halts-bronx-train-thursday-morning/

Hicksville Fire: *News 12 Bronx,* "Volunteers protest demolition of Hicksville home, claim cats are still stuck inside," February 5, 2024 https://bronx.news12.com/volunteers-protest-demolition-of-hicksville-home-claim-cats-are-still-stuck-inside

Made in United States
Cleveland, OH
03 June 2025